engaging young writers

Preschool–Grade 1

Matt Glover

HEINEMANN
Portsmouth, NH

Heinemann
361 Hanover Street
Portsmouth, NH 03801–3912
www.heinemann.com

Offices and agents throughout the world

Library of Congress Cataloging-in-Publication Data
Glover, Matt.
    Engaging young writers : preschool–grade 1 / Matt Glover.
        p. cm.
    Includes bibliographical references and index.
    ISBN 13: 978-0-325-01745-7
    ISBN 10: 0-325-01745-X
    1. English language—Composition and exercises—Study and teaching (Early childhood).   I. Title.
    LB1139.5.L35G59   2009
    372.62′3—dc22   2008048254

Editor: Kate Montgomery
Production: Elizabeth Valway
Cover photography: D.A. Fleischer
Cover design: Bernadette Skok
Composition: House of Equations, Inc.
Manufacturing: Louise Richardson

Printed in the United States of America on acid-free paper
19   VP   11

To Bridget

Contents

Foreword

■ ■

As teachers, we live narrative lives. Dozens of little interwoven stories play out in our classrooms each day as we live and learn alongside children. Some stories last only a few moments—the bird that lands on the windowsill and sings just long enough and just loud enough to draw everyone's attention, then lifts up and flies away. Short stories that make us smile at their memory. Other stories unfold for days and weeks before their endings come at last, and some are left unfinished even as the school year comes to a close. When we look back and remember a year in a classroom, it's the stories we hold onto, and the themes of those stories that give color and texture to our memories.

Matt Glover pays attention to stories. When I was first getting to know him, he sent me stories—two, three, or six a week. If we had shared an office or worked at the same school instead of being separated by several hundred miles, I'm sure he would have just popped in to tell me these stories. Instead he emailed, and my inbox filled with them until I had to make Matt his own folder. I titled it "Matt's stories."

Matt's stories were always about writing and he gathered them as he spent time in preschool and kindergarten classrooms at the school where he is principal. While the characters, settings, and plots changed, Matt's stories always had basically the same theme: young children are capable of remarkable thinking when they have paper and markers in hand. Every single story, same theme. But instead of becoming bored by this sameness in Matt's stories, I became intrigued.

I was intrigued by the children and their thinking, and I wondered about the potential for richer teaching that might come from studying very young children's first efforts as writers. This intrigue led Matt and I to collaborate on this very study and, later, to write about it in a book we co-authored. But I was equally intrigued by Matt's ability to see so much in the story of a single interaction with a child. Matt didn't sit down next to children who were writing just to talk to them; he sat down next to them to learn something from them. He struck me then (and continues to strike me now) as the consummate narrative learner who does the rigorous, intellectual work he needs to do to find meaning in every interaction he has with children.

In *Engaging Young Writers*, Matt shares with us so much of what he knows and understands about the writing of very young children. We get to peer over his shoulder and be narrative learners, too, as we live out stories with him in classrooms, stories that lead again and again to important ideas and foundational understandings. Examples of children's writing fill the pages of this book, bringing the stories of the children who wrote them to life. Of course, Matt reminds us often that the written products really don't mean that much if we don't look at the writers who created them.

The topic of this book is an important one. Throughout its pages, Matt helps teachers think very specifically about finding ways to help young children gravitate toward writing, exploring a variety of what he calls *entry points* for children into writing. As he explains these different entry points, it's clear that Matt is interested in helping children find motivation for writing, but he is equally interested in practices that help children believe they are capable as writers. And significantly, the larger point of the book is that children will come to the table as writers with different motivations and interests. There is no one right path on which all children need begin their journeys as writers. There are multiple paths.

As teachers, we do indeed live narrative lives, and if you read *Engaging Young Writers*, Matt will help you live out new kinds of stories with the children you teach. I know he's helped me do just that. I'm a better teacher because of what I've learned from him.

—Katie Wood Ray

Acknowledgments

■ ■

This book focuses on entry points into writing for young children, and adults have entry points into writing as well. I am fortunate to have had two amazing people who acted as entry points for my writing life, Katie Ray and Kate Montgomery.

None of the learning I have done about writing with young children would have happened without Katie Ray. I've had the gift of learning about thinking and writing from a truly amazing educator and writer. Katie encouraged me to write on my own and nurtured my early writing attempts. She also responded thoughtfully to drafts of this book and struck the right balance of thoughtful questions and encouragement. Thank you, Katie, for being such a supportive friend.

I was incredibly lucky to have Kate Montgomery as my editor on this project. Kate's support and constant encouragement were crucial in nurturing my emerging self-image as a writer. Kate saw me as an author before I did. Her many suggestions, especially the focus on entry points, made this a more cohesive book. I so appreciate her gentle suggestions, positive feedback, and enthusiasm for the ideas in this book. Thank you, Kate, for your vision and guidance.

Thank you to the many people at Heinemann who were supportive of this project and helped bring it to fruition. Thank you to Elizabeth Valway for all of her guidance and patience and to Vicki Boyd for providing opportunities for me to learn.

I am fortunate to work with and learn from incredibly talented teachers at Creekside Early Childhood School. This book is reflective of their collective work. I'd like to thank all of the teachers who taught at Creekside during the 2007–8 school year. Preschool teachers: Susan Bolander, Cindy Brausch-Knemeyer, Beth Carver, Penny Cecil, Cheryl Fuertges, Pam Heidorn, Joanne Muir-Myers, Chris Piepmeier, Pat Schmees, and Keri Turner. Kindergarten teachers: April Bruder, Danine Gebhart, Leslie Herald, Shannon Henderson, Stacey Hodson, Janet

Raulin, Jackie Schallip, Lisa Smallwood, and Sherry Stoffer. First-grade teachers: Stephanie Allan, Danielle Beneteau, Marlene Cooley, Kaelin Goode, Jami Fisher, Dawn Galvin, Danielle Henschen, Amanda Johnson, Cathy Johnson, Darby Morris, Penny Musser, Jessica Rostron, Lauren Seal, Gloria Sprague, and Amy Winkle. Specialists: Jana Borgemenke, Angie Bryant, Sharon Byrnes, Emily De-Salvo, Sherry Federle, Sara Fiedler, April Grahl, Angela Hott, Diane Keene, Carol Ryan, Joyce Smith, Patty Swanson, Vinnie Taneja, Megan Walters, Peg Wernersbach, and Emily Yount. Thank you for thinking so deeply about children. Special thanks go to Shannon Henderson for her thoughts and work with connecting dramatic play and writing in kindergarten.

I would also like to thank the teachers and specialists whom I've worked with at Shawnee Early Childhood School: Melissa Adolph, Heather Chaney, Kate Doyle, Susan Farnell, Patty Geroni, Natalie Messer, Mara Osterfeld, Cara Pease, and Cindy Trimbell. Many of the stories and ideas in this book originated in their amazing classrooms.

Most of the ideas in this book can be traced back to conversations with Creekside Literacy Specialists Mary Alice Berry, Mari Pumphrey, Asha Ruiz, Laura Sites, and Emily Speed. Thank you for your expertise and passion. Thanks especially to Mary Alice and Asha for helping me find the essential words.

I have learned so much from Pat Mascaritolo's and Peggy Banet's leadership. Their advocacy for children is a constant reminder of our priorities. Thank you to Amy Fugate for making the final days of writing this book possible.

Bobbie Bach, Chris Caster, Tara Eddy, and Kathy Keyes make everything at Creekside run like clockwork. Thank you for making sure that children remain at the heart of our school.

The teachers at Lads and Lassies Preschool, Stacy Akers, Valerie Barrett, Sharon Marck, and Cindi Wetzel, allowed me to volunteer in their classrooms, let me learn alongside them, and never made me feel like "that parent."

I was fortunate throughout the writing of this book to have conversations with amazing educators. Kathy Collins helped me understand that the doubts and anxieties I was facing as an author were common. Renee Dinnerstein listened and responded thoughtfully to ideas about inquiry, curriculum, and units of study. Stephanie Jones shared insightful feedback on *Already Ready* (Ray and Glover 2008) and helped me keep in mind the range of student experiences in early childhood classrooms and homes. Ellin Keene helped me think through issues of depth in Chapter 1, and Isoke Nia shared insights into her thinking about list books and storybooks. Thanks to all of you for your encouraging words and helping me ponder important ideas.

I want to thank the teachers and administrators who have invited me to come and talk about writing in their schools and districts. The more I spoke about the ideas in this book, the easier it was to write about them. Thank you for letting me try out new ideas and for responding so thoughtfully. Thank you especially to all of the teachers who have shared questions and success stories about young writers.

My niece Kate Apfelbeck is a talented writer. Thank you, Kate, for making the last few weeks especially entertaining, and thank you for the lemonade.

My children, Harrison, Meredith, Natalie, and Molly, provided inspiration for many of the ideas contained in this book. Thank you for being so patient and understanding, and for being such interesting thinkers.

Finally, this book is really a joint effort with my "saint of a wife," Bridget. Bridget listened and provided insightful suggestions before any words were written, and she managed to keep everything in our lives afloat while I wrote. Thank you for your support and love.

Introduction

■■■

Until recently in my professional life, I didn't think of myself as a writer. It wasn't that I disliked writing, but if I had been in a room full of people and someone had said, "Raise your hand if you are a writer," my hand would have stayed down. To write this book, I had to bridge the gap between my passion for teaching writing to young children and seeing myself as someone who could write a book. I needed to develop my image of myself as a writer.

Like young writers, I had influences that prompted my entry into writing. I had a deep interest in how young children are invited into the writing process. I also had a compelling purpose to write: to share what I was learning with early childhood educators. Having an interest and purpose were instrumental in getting me to start.

Why am I starting off with this bit of self-analysis? Because the process I went through mirrors in many ways what children experience as they enter into writing. I needed someone to nudge, not push, my development. I needed someone to honor my early approximations of professional writing. And I needed someone who believed I could write before I did. By examining the process I went through in creating my own image of myself as a writer, I have come to better understand what young students experience as they enter into writing.

Engaging Young Writers grew out of a book that Katie Ray and I wrote together titled *Already Ready: Nurturing Writers in Preschool and Kindergarten* (2008). At the end of *Already Ready*, there were more ideas that we wanted to examine in greater depth. One of those ideas was how adults invite young children into writing. While some of the stories about students in *Already Ready* were related to issues of motivation and energy for writing, I wanted to explore the idea of entry points into writing in greater detail.

I use the term *entry points* to describe invitations and motivations for young writers. Children write for many reasons, and those reasons are each connected to an entry point. For example, it might be that a child has meaningful information he wants to share, that he is writing for a particular audience, or that a teacher has invited him to write. When teachers and parents deliberately provide children with a variety of entry points, taking into account how and why they are asking children to write, they can positively influence children's attitudes and dispositions toward writing, and in turn help students grow as skilled writers.

To understand the experiences described and the student writing you will see in this book, it will help to know a bit about the school where I work and my role in the school. I am the principal at Creekside Early Childhood School, a public school of more than nine hundred preschool, kindergarten, and first-grade students in the Lakota Local School District, located north of Cincinnati, Ohio. Our preschool population is very diverse in terms of the range of abilities. Half of our preschool students are children with identified disabilities and half are children who display typical development. While our preschool children's chronological ages are mostly three and four, developmentally they are anywhere from six months to six years of age. Our students in kindergarten and first grade represent a more natural population in terms of percentage of students with disabilities. Our beliefs about writing and instructional strategies span the range of ages and abilities in our school.

I teach in classrooms frequently, although not nearly as much as I would like. Some of the stories about young writers that appear in this book occurred while I was teaching writing in a class, so I understand them more as a teacher than as a principal. Other stories occurred in classrooms when I wasn't there, so I understand them more as a principal studying young children's writing. Either way, it's important to note that these are stories that occurred naturally in our school and are an outgrowth of teachers' work with young writers.

Entry Points into Writing

Throughout this book we'll look at the many ways teachers can provide young writers with engaging entry points into writing. Entry points provide motivation and energy for writing. Energy for writing affects student interest, attitude, stamina, and desire for writing.

Chapter 1 provides an overview of important big ideas for writing with young children. Ellin Keene has said that rewriting and rereading are really forms of rethinking, so even if you've read *Already Ready*, this chapter will help deepen your understanding of these big ideas for young writers and provide a conceptual basis for the rest of the book.

Chapter 2 describes the concept of entry points in more detail and introduces the five types of entry points highlighted in this book: essential, invitational, story, experience, and interest. Each of these entry points influences children's motivation and energy for writing.

Chapter 3 examines three entry points that are essential for young writers: meaning, choice, and purpose. These are not new issues in learning or teaching writing, but they play a crucial role in young writers' development.

Chapter 4 looks at how teachers invite children into writing. Since that occurs differently in preschool and in the primary grades, the chapter starts with an explanation of some key similarities and differences between teaching writing in preschool and in kindergarten and first grade. It then looks at how preschool teachers invite children into writing through conversations and how kindergarten and first-grade teachers invite children into writing within the structure of writing workshop and units of study.

Chapters 5, 6, and 7 look at three specific entry points: story, experience, and interest. Chapter 5 examines the potential role of dramatic play and favorite books in sparking writing, while Chapter 6 looks at how children's experiences can lead to writing topics. Finally, Chapter 7 focuses on the possibilities for nonfiction writing when teachers capitalize on student interest.

A Note About Students' Books

Throughout this book you will notice that some of the student-produced books include typed text to go along with each page. It's important to note that the typed text never appeared on the students' actual books. The only purpose in including it here is so that you can read the books exactly the same way the students read them originally. The text represents the students' oral readings of their books. If the children were able to read their books to you, you wouldn't need the text, but since we don't have a Play button that you can press to hear children read their stories (wouldn't that be cool), we'll have to settle for the written text.

Supporting Teachers Across Early Childhood

This book is intended to support teachers who work with young children in preschool, kindergarten, and first grade. At times it focuses more on one group or the other, but I encourage you to read all of the sections of this book for several reasons.

@ The underlying concepts of writing are the same for preschool, kindergarten, and first-grade writers. Similarly, most of the strategies, ideas, and suggestions represent effective teaching for all young children.

@ While the underlying concepts are the same, there are significant developmental differences between preschoolers and the primary-grade children. Therefore, the structure of writing instruction looks different with each age group. It is important for teachers to understand these developmental and structural differences.

@ Some preschool children are more like kindergarten and first-grade students, and some kindergartners and first graders have needs that are more similar to preschool students. Because you will have a wide range of student needs in your class, you must understand aspects of child development beyond just the particular grade you teach.

@ In order to meet children's individual needs as writers, we must recognize what they can do independently and determine the next small step in their writing development. Once a teacher identifies what a child can do independently, she can determine what the next incremental step in his writing development is and decide on an appropriate teaching point, based on her knowledge of early childhood writing development. As teachers, we need an understanding of where a child has been and where he is going.

As you read you will notice that some chapters have separate sections for preschool and the primary grades while in other chapters the two groups are intermixed. In chapters where there is a significant difference between strategies that support preschool and primary writers, I have separated them, such as in the discussion of dramatic play in Chapter 5. In the chapters where the strategies are more similar, such as writing about interests (Chapter 7), the preschool and primary-grade examples are interspersed. My hope is that first-grade teachers will find the preschool examples as enlightening as the first-grade examples can be for preschool teachers.

Every Child

Finally, while the concepts about writing and entry points hold true across age and grade-level groupings, they also hold true across other characteristics of students. The strategies and practices described in the following chapters are appropriate for students regardless of gender, ethnicity, socioeconomic status, or ability level. I occasionally encounter "yeah, but" comments about young writers. They go something like "Yeah, but my children don't have those types of experiences to write about" or "Yeah, but my students need the basic skills before they can think about composition." In my experience these "yeah, but" comments don't have to be true for children. The stories about students and their writing that appear in the chapters that follow represent a range of characteristics and abilities in young writers. What the kids do have in common are teachers who value student engagement and a school environment that values teacher decision making based on the individual needs of each child.

Big Ideas for Nurturing Young Writers

It was late summer as I walked down the hallway into a preschool class to teach writing for the first time one school year. The freshness of the new year was evident as I watched three- and four-year-olds tumble into their classrooms. Since school had been in session for only a couple of weeks, I wasn't expecting that the children in this class would have done much writing this early in the year. I soon found out how wrong I was.

As I entered the room, I was greeted by several children who wanted to tell me about all sorts of things, including telling me about books they had made. Tommy excitedly told me about a soccer trophy he had brought to show his friends. I asked him where the trophy was and learned that his teacher had already suggested that he could make a book about his trophy, and he had put his trophy in the writing center so he could write about it later in the day. Tommy retrieved the trophy, showed it to me, and then returned it to the writing center, where it stayed, waiting to be written about later in the day.

After talking with students informally for a bit, we started talking about writing as we usually do, with a read-aloud. On this day the book was *Wemberly Worried*, by Kevin Henkes (2000). We discussed the fact that authors sometimes write books about friends and that preschoolers can make books about friends, too.

    Matt: Kevin Henkes wrote this book about this girl Wemberly, who was worried about going to school, and how she made a new friend. Sometimes people make books about things that are important to them, like their friends and their families.

    Justin: I made a book about my mom and dad and sister.

Shawna: I made a book about my dog.

Matt: You both made books about things that are important to you, just like Kevin Henkes wrote a book about making friends. Some of you could write about things that are important to you today.

Antonio: I'm going to make a book about my baby brother.

Other students talked about possible book topics, and then the read-aloud was over.

After the read-aloud, students went off to engage in a variety of activities in the classroom, with writing being just one of many choices. In our classrooms, students typically have about an hour of choice time in which they choose to participate in various activities in the classroom. Teachers integrate themselves into these activities as well as inviting children to engage in particular activities. I soon found Elijah at the science table examining a pumpkin, complete with stems and leaves, that he had brought in from home. There was also a picture of the pumpkin from his garden at home. Elijah told me about pumpkins in great detail, explaining how pumpkins grow on a vine and change color as they get bigger. At the end of our conversation I asked if he might make a book that would teach people about pumpkins, since he obviously knew a lot about them. He said, "Sure, right after I play cars with Tommy."

Next Kaylee came over to the writing table. Kaylee was in preschool the year before so I knew her as a writer. As Kaylee got out a blank book and grabbed a marker, I asked her, "What are you going to write about today?"

"Cats . . . again," Kaylee replied confidently. This two-word answer spoke volumes about how Kaylee saw herself as a writer. She saw herself as the type of child who wrote books frequently, who often wrote about cats, and who was good at it. She clearly saw herself as an author. For Kaylee, making a book so early in the year was as natural as choosing any other activity in the classroom.

When Kaylee finished her cat book, Elijah decided to come and make his pumpkin book (see Figure 1.1). While Elijah was writing, Tommy came over and sat right in front of his soccer trophy to make his book about playing soccer. If you could see Tommy's trophy, you would recognize all of the parts of the trophy represented on the first page of his book. Tommy and Elijah worked on their books fairly independently, and their finished books looked like they were made by three- and four-year-olds, which makes sense of course since they were three and four years old. For Kaylee, Tommy, and Elijah and the other students in their class, making books was a regular part of what they did at school.

Engaging Young Writers focuses on the teacher decisions and classroom environments that prompt writers like Elijah, Tommy, and Kaylee to write so easily so

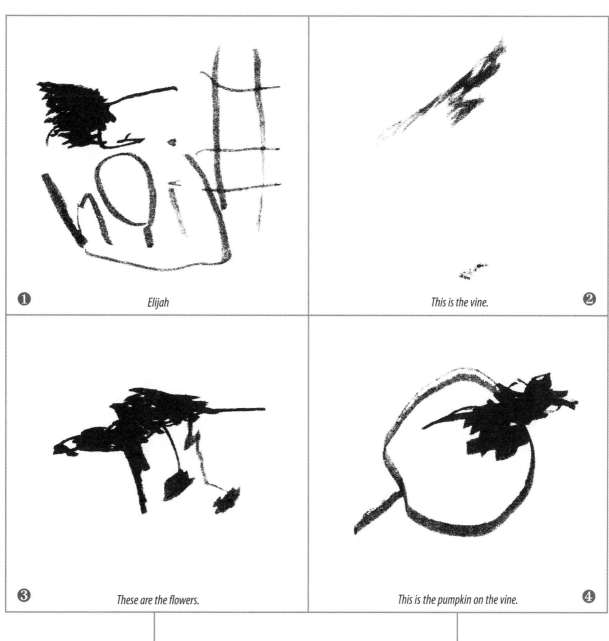

① *Elijah*

② *This is the vine.*

③ *These are the flowers.*

④ *This is the pumpkin on the vine.*

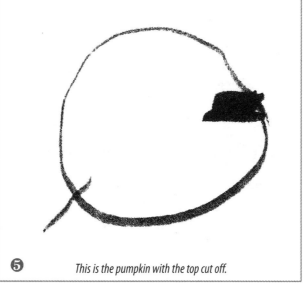

⑤ *This is the pumpkin with the top cut off.*

FIG. 1.1 **Elijah's Book About Pumpkins**

early in the year. What conditions help young writers successfully enter into the writing process? Why do young children want to write? How can teachers help children see writing as a natural part of their lives? How do teachers invite children to the table to write? These are all questions of motivation. Teachers have a huge impact on children's motivation to do all sorts of things in the classroom, including their motivation to write.

Throughout this book I refer to young children's *writing*. It's important to note that writing encompasses a wide range of products—from writing that consists almost entirely of pictures in preschool to writing that is fairly conventional in first grade. Some of the writing is very approximated, which is entirely appropriate since it has been written by inexperienced writers. Children's approximations for words can include scribble writing, random strings of letters, marks that look a bit like letters, or actual letters that correspond to the sounds they hear when saying words slowly. The key is that regardless of whether there are words on the page or not, or how approximated the writing appears, the child is conveying a thought through symbols and pictures on a page and is therefore writing.

Big Ideas for Young Writers

In order to look at issues of motivation for writing, we must first look briefly at the key concepts related to the teaching of writing and to learning with young children. This philosophical underpinning is crucial to understanding the interactions of teachers and young writers. These concepts are also crucial to understanding the focus of this book on the thinking, or composition, aspect of writing. Writing conventions, spelling, and grammar are important but are certainly not enough by themselves to help children become strong writers. These big ideas of writing with young children are

- fostering children's images of themselves as writers;

- honoring approximations;

- nudging rather than pushing;

- understanding vision: the importance of making books;

- teaching children to read like writers; and

- understanding dimensions of composition development.

These certainly aren't the only concepts that are important, but they provide a solid foundation for teacher decisions regarding what to do, and what not to do, with young writers. These concepts are explored in depth in *Already Ready: Nurturing Young Writers in Preschool and Kindergarten* (Ray and Glover 2008). Before we can look at issues related to motivation and entry points for young writers, we must first understand the conditions that existed in Kaylee, Tommy, and Elijah's classroom.

Recognizing the Thinking Aspect of Writing

Young children are capable of remarkable thinking, especially when they are engaged in experiences that foster their intellectual growth as well as their academic growth. Much of what is written about supporting very young writers focuses on the academic aspect of writing through topics such as phonemic awareness, letter-sound relationships, and letter formation. Much less is written about the thinking aspect of writing. While the conventions are important, teachers must also look at the intellectual, thinking side of writing.

Allison's book about her birthday shows evidence of strong thinking as an author. Allison was a kindergartner when she wrote this book early in the year. A typical kindergarten book about a birthday party, if it were written as a book rather than as one page in a journal, might go something like this:

> It was my birthday.
> We went bowling.
> We ate cake.
> We went home.

You can see where Allison's book sounds very different (see Figure 1.2). Her use of pairs of adjectives, such as *rolling* and *bowling*, is not what you might typically expect to see early in the year in kindergarten. Her words like *scrumptious* and phrases like *filled our bellies* sound like they're coming from a much more experienced writer. You can clearly see how Allison was trying to write descriptively and with specific detail as she was thinking like a writer.

The thing is, the sophistication of Allison's writing is not surprising if you understand the teaching that was going on in her kindergarten classroom. Her teacher had been helping students look at how authors use beautiful language in their books and had suggested that they might try to do that in their writing. They had been reading books like *My Mama Had a Dancing Heart* during read-aloud and had noticed how Libba Moore Gray (1995) uses language in this beautiful book (see example on page 7).

FIG. 1.2 *Alison's Book About Her Birthday*

My mamma had a dancing heart
and she shared that heart with me.
With a grin and a giggle,
A hug and a whistle we'd slap our knees
and Mama would say:
"Bless the world
it feels like a tip-tapping,
song-singing
finger-snapping kind of day.
Let's celebrate!"
And so we did.

Allison had been hearing language like "tip-tapping, song-singing . . . kind of day" and talking with her class about the decisions Libba Moore Gray made, which makes it easy to see why Allison wrote, "It was minty and scrumptious and the greatest chocolate. It filled our bellies."

There are certainly things we could learn from an examination of Allison's use of writing conventions. We can see clear evidence that Allison knew a lot about consonant blends and high-frequency words. We could also note that she has only a couple of lowercase letters and that there is no end punctuation. If Allison's teacher had focused only on conventions in her teaching or had talked with Allison only about conventions in her writing, she would have missed out on the incredible thinking that Allison was so clearly capable of displaying. Fortunately for Allison, her teacher valued Allison's thinking as a writer.

With very young children who are just starting to learn about letters and sounds, if we focus only on the academic side of writing, there may not be a lot to look at. They may not produce anything that resembles conventional writing and even their pictures may not be very representational. If those children don't have the opportunity to show their thinking through very approximated writing, whether it's scribble writing, random letters, or beginning phonetic spelling, we miss out as teachers and parents on some pretty amazing thinking. It's this type of thinking that is going to help them be successful, both as writers and thinkers, as they go through school and life. So let's take a look at the big ideas that support children as thinkers and writers.

Fostering Children's Images of Themselves as Writers

If you were to walk into a preschool classroom and give two three-year-old children blank books and markers and ask them to make books, it would not be uncommon to get two very different reactions from each child. One might very likely say, "Sure," and start putting marks on the book. It could be just as likely that the other child would react in the exact opposite way and would say, "I don't know how to write," or "I don't know how to make a book." In some schools it would not be uncommon for a child to respond to the question by saying, "My teacher writes the words," or "My mom could help me do it." There are a couple of questions that naturally follow:

- Why does one three-year-old have an image of himself as someone who can make a book and another child does not?

- What interactions influence and strengthen either disposition?

We know that bookmaking does not need to appear to be a difficult endeavor for a child. Recently I had the opportunity to teach in a preschool class composed of three-year-old children at Whitney Young Early Childhood Center in Fort Wayne, Indiana. This was the first time I had met these students and the first time they had the opportunity to make books. The goal for my introductory read-aloud was to share the idea that "people make books and you can, too." After the read-aloud I told the children that I would be at the writing center that day and that hopefully I would get to see some of them make books that day. Literally five minutes later, fourteen of the seventeen children in the class were at the writing area, and several other tables, making books. Of course, I realize that a large part of their motivation was that I was a novelty in the room and that there were many adults watching what was going on. What was significant, however, was how easily they started making books. Some children made books that had only pictures about familiar topics, like families and friends. Others used various types of approximated writing and made books about topics of interest such as TV shows and sports. It simply wasn't that difficult, and now that they were started, the teacher's job was to begin strengthening their images of themselves as writers.

In order for bookmaking to be a meaningful experience for children and not just one that they are complying with, children must seem themselves as authors, as people who make books. Just as a dancer must see herself as someone who can dance or as a painter must see himself as someone who can paint, young children must believe that they are the type of people who can make a book.

Young children generally have a fairly easy time envisioning themselves as many different things. They think of themselves as astronauts and princesses in an imaginary way, but they see themselves as dinosaur experts or expert builders just as easily. Fortunately, they can also envision themselves as writers, which is crucial at any age if you are going to write.

At some point early in their lives, children do see themselves as writers. If you give a very young child of one or two years some blank paper and markers, she will eagerly attack the paper and see what happens. Then as they get older and we give them blank books, kids will generally put something on each page and make a book. However, that is not always the case. Sometimes children lose this image at an early age, seeing writing as something that only older people can do. When people, again, at any age, don't see themselves as writers, writing can be a difficult, frustrating endeavor.

Evan, a first grader, had a particularly strong image of himself as an author. Evan and his classmates had been studying authors' notes in the back of books and had noticed that these notes often include a picture of the author. Evan was particularly taken with this idea and decided he wanted a picture of himself for the author's note in the voluminous Pokémon book that he had been writing. He noticed that some authors, like Shel Silverstein, looked very serious in their photos, so Evan decided that his recent school photo just wouldn't work. After practicing his best Shel Silverstein pose at school, Evan went home and asked his father to take his photograph. The photo was taken in the "fancy room" at home (the living room), which seemed to have the appropriate tone for this serious occasion. If you grab a copy of *A Light in the Attic* and look at the photo of Shel Silverstein (1981) on the back cover, you will see the similarities between Evan's author's note photo (see Figure 1.3) and Shel's.

While this is a cute, endearing story, it is also much more than that. It provides an important vision of a child having a strong image of himself as being just like a published author. This vision is crucial if children are going to believe they can write and make books.

A sure sign of whether a child views himself as a writer is simply to give him some blank pages stapled together and ask him if he will make a book. Children who see themselves as writers will go off and make a book, while others will say they can't or that they will need someone to do the writing for them.

Honoring Approximations

Since much of very young children's writing is going to be very approximated and nonrepresentational, adults and children must honor and feel comfortable with these approximations. As adults, we have to be willing to take a child's piece of writing and see all that the child can do, not what she can't. So often it is easy for adults to miss the incredible thinking that is evidenced in very young children's writing simply because it is hard to tell what's going on just from the illustrations. Elijah's pumpkin book, appearing earlier in this chapter (see Figure 1.1), is a good example of a book that has tremendous thinking taking place, which is evident if you look beyond the illustrations and listen to the child.

FIG. 1.3 *Evan's Author Page*

The result of adults feeling comfortable with children's approximations is that children will feel more comfortable with their own approximations. The hope is that every child will feel as comfortable with her writing as four-year-old Katie did one day when she was reading a book she wrote to her teacher. As she read the first page she pointed to her scribble writing and said, "This says Beautiful Jewelry Shop. You would know that if you were me." What a wonderful sense of "I'm four; this is the best I can write it." Katie clearly showed her teacher that she realized she was the only one who knew what it said because she wrote it and that she realized her teacher couldn't independently read her approximations. Most importantly, it showed Katie's level of comfort with that arrangement being normal and acceptable. Our hope as adults should be that all children feel so comfortable with their approximations.

Of course, if adults are honoring children's approximations, there is no need for adults to write for children or for adults to write something for children to copy.

If we truly believe that kids are writers, then there is no need to write for them, especially when a child has initiated the writing. This idea is explored much more in depth in Chapter 5 of *Already Ready* (Ray and Glover 2008), but here a few quick reasons why children should do their own writing.

- If a child can't read conventional writing, then the conventional writing that an adult writes in his book does not help him reread what he has written.

- If an adult is doing the writing for a child, then we have no idea what kind of writing the child can do all on her own. And, if we don't know what a child can do on her own, then we don't know what to teach her. Action and observation are the starting points of assessment, which in turn should be the starting point for teaching.

- If adults are writing for a child, we run the risk of jumping the child ahead in developmental stages and outside his zone of proximal development. For most preschool students, conventional writing represents a large push forward rather than a small nudge just beyond their current writing approximations.

- If adults write for children, we are sending the message that children aren't really writers, that only adults can do the real writing work. If we truly believe children are writers, we shouldn't send a mixed message that tells them they are writers, but not really.

By having repeated experiences with adults nudging them toward writing on their own, children will develop the sense of comfort that four-year-old Natalie has. Natalie is by nature a perfectionist and wants things to be right. But over time, Natalie has grown comfortable with not knowing how to spell things. Natalie will now ask, "How do you spell *dear?*" and, before you can answer, say, "Wait, I'll just write it my best four-year-old way." Of course, if she's going to write it, that's really all she can do, so it's important that she feels comfortable with that understanding.

Nudging Rather Than Pushing

The idea of nudging versus pushing is kind of like a small tugboat pushing a much larger freighter in a harbor. If the tugboat gets a running start and tries to motor up quickly and push the ship, there will be little effect, other than perhaps smashing the tugboat. However, if the tugboat provides little nudges over time, the ship will move.

Most people learn best when what they are trying to learn is just a little bit harder than what they can do easily on their own, especially if there is a more experienced person nearby to help. When my son, Harrison, was eleven years old, we took him and his sisters to a wedding for the first time. After the wedding we went to the reception and as soon as the DJ started playing music, my then eight-year-old daughter Meredith (who, like her mother, Bridget, has never met a stranger) hit the dance floor, ready for action. Soon Bridget and Meredith were dancing away, while Harrison and I were with most of the other dads and sons, sitting at the tables on the other side of the room. As we watched the dancing, I figured that if there was going to be a male Glover dancing that night, it would have to be Harrison, so I asked him if he was going to go dance with his mom and sister. After thinking it over for a minute, Harrison joined them on the dance floor for his first dancing experience. From across the room I could see Bridget talking to Harrison and could imagine what she was saying. Later that night she confirmed that my guesses were pretty accurate. The conversation went something like this.

As Harrison stood, stiff legged, hands by his side, in the middle of the dance floor, Bridget said, "OK, Harrison, you need to bend your knees a bit." And Harrison unrhythmically bent his knees.

"All right, great, now you have to sway a bit from side to side." And Harrison started swaying from side to side, bobbing up and down.

"Wonderful. Now, you have to bring your arms up and move them." Harrison bent his arms ever so slightly, careful not to draw too much attention.

And so the dance lesson progressed. Mind you, without the context of the dance floor, music, and other dancers, you might never know that his actions were dancing, but as Peter Reynolds in his book *Ish* (2004) would say, Harrison's movements were dancing-ish. And that's all that was important for his first dance experience—that with a bit of adult support, he could do a little more dancing than he could before.

Bridget knew that to teach Harrison she had to first see what he could do independently and figure out what he could do with a *bit* of adult support. Bridget's supportive nudging was aligned to just what Harrison needed next. She observed what he was doing on the dance floor (standing still) and nudged him to the next small step on the dancing continuum (bending your knees). As soon as he reached that next benchmark, she nudged some more. She could have easily made the mistake of giving him too much instruction at once and caused her tentative dance student to feel that dancing was out of his reach. Her small, gentle nudges helped move his learning along.

The important thing for dancers or young writers is that what they are being asked and encouraged to do is just within their reach. As adults we must be able to see what a child can do independently and what he can do with a bit of support. If we don't know what a child can do on his own, then we don't know what's best to teach him next.

Understanding Vision: The Importance of Making Books

You will notice that the writing examples you see in this book are primarily of books that children have made. That is because at our school the primary type of writing young children are doing is making books rather than writing in a journal or on a single piece of paper. By books, I simply mean four or five pieces of blank paper stapled together. The reason for making books is simple. Books are what children have the greatest vision for, and having a clear vision for what you are making is important in any act of composition. Young children have the clearest vision for making picture books because that is the type of writing they have seen the most. Even if they haven't had many experiences with books at home, they should have had numerous opportunities to see and hear books each day in early childhood classrooms.

When children have a clear vision for what they are making, it is easy for them to go make it, especially if they are comfortable with the fact that their book is going to look like it was made by a three-year-old or a six-year-old. "Go make one of these" isn't a difficult proposition for these children (Ray and Glover 2008).

Sometimes teachers have the perception that making a book is too difficult for a very young child. However, in the contexts I am describing, it is no more difficult for a child to make a book than it is to write on a single piece of paper, assuming we understand and honor their approximations of what a book looks like and how it works. For example, when we look at a published picture book, we take for granted that all of the pages will be connected to the central idea of the book. Young children may not understand that or yet be able to accomplish that level of writing. That's OK. If a student has a book of disconnected ideas on each page, it gives us a good idea of what we might nudge her to over time. In the meantime, we honor and accept her book the same way we do another child's book that does have connected ideas. The key is that we know to teach them this only by watching what they do independently when given a blank book and asked to make a book.

Teaching Children to Read Like Writers

As children move through the elementary grades they should be expected to read like writers. That is, teachers should expect them to learn how to write well by studying what published authors do as they write in compelling ways. People often don't think about very young children reading like writers. However, it makes perfect sense that they do, since young children are great noticers of all sorts of things in their world. I'm sadly reminded of this every time a four-year-old asks where my hair is or immediately notices (and points out) when I make a mistake. It's natural, then, that they also notice things in books. For example, I had read the book *Too Many Pears!* by Jackie French (2003) to older children and I'd never noticed that Pamela, the cow, has a spot shaped like a pear. But the first time I read it to a preschool class, the children noticed right away.

Young children notice the things we point out in books, and they notice many things we never point out at all. Isabella noticed something all on her own and then tried it out in her book. When you first look at Isabella's book (see Figure 1.4), you'll probably appreciate the charming story about the snowman but wonder about the purpose of the first page with all of the scribble writing. Isabella had noticed that when her teacher read a book, she usually skipped the page with the publisher, copyright, and so on. So, she included one of these pages in her book. When she got to this page while reading it to the class, she simply said, "This is the page you don't read," and then kept going. She noticed what writers do and did the same thing on her own—clear evidence of reading like a writer.

Understanding Dimensions of Composition Development

As teachers sit down side by side with a child and talk about his writing, they are always thinking about what they are going to teach this child, in a very nudging kind of way. There are two broad realms from which they can select their teaching point:

@ the word-making realm of writing: spelling, letter formation, conventions, mechanics of writing

@ the composition, thinking, realm of writing

Both realms are important and teachers will select points from each realm over the course of many teaching interactions. Let's briefly consider each writing realm.

Word-Making Development

Typically, much of the writing work done with young children is focused on how print works. It is helpful to understand the stages of word making, or spelling

FIG. 1.4 *Isabella's Book About a Snowman*

development. There are numerous resources that describe the stages of word-making development through which children usually progress. Those stages generally include

- scribble writing

- mock letters

- random strings of letters

- beginning phonetic or invented spelling

In addition to spelling development, teachers might nudge students to use spaces between words, grammar, or punctuation. All of these nudging points are important ones for children to eventually master so that their writing can be read easily by others.

Composition Development

Composition development refers to the thinking children are engaged in when they are composing writing. Composition can refer to how the child is planning out her book, what she will include (and what she will leave out), and how she will write her book.

In many ways composition development is much more difficult to see and support than word-making development. Spelling and punctuation are usually easy to work on because they're so evident. If we think back to Allison's birthday book, we can quickly find things to nudge her on, such as using lowercase letters, in part because they are so easy to identify. But where do we nudge Allison if we choose to nudge her composition? The composition aspect of writing can be more difficult to see, especially with very young children.

There are a number of questions we can use to look at a child's writing to determine where to nudge his composition growth. Figure 1.5 details dimensions of composition development. The purpose in showing these composition dimensions here is to highlight the difference between word-making and composition development.

A Web of Learning

In these types of classrooms, children have images of themselves as writers. These students are guided by teachers who honor their writing approximations, observe

Composition Dimensions

Understandings About Books

@ Is this child's book about something?

@ How has the child organized this book? Does it move through time (narrative) or through a list of ideas (nonnarrative)?

@ When the child reads the book, does it sound like a book?

@ Does the child read the book basically the same way over time?

@ Is the child making this book in the manner of other picture books he's seen?

@ What does this book show the child understands about genre?

@ How is the child representing meaning in this book?

Understandings About Process

@ Is the child intentional about what she is representing on the page?

@ Does the child engage in revision while composing a picture book?

@ Is there any evidence the child is thinking ahead about what he'll write?

@ Has the child made any intentional crafting decisions in this book?

@ How long has the child worked on this book? In one sitting? Over time?

@ Does the writer show a willingness to solve problems as she writes?

Understandings About What It Means to Be a Writer

@ How (and why) has the child decided what to write about in this book?

@ How interested is the child in an audience's response to the book?

@ Has the child composed in a way that has led her to new meaning as she has written?

@ Can I see in this book that the child has been willing to take compositional risks?

@ As I interact with this child around this book, does it seem he has a sense of self a writer? A sense of history?

@ Does the child show she understands her powerful position as author of the book?

FIG. 1.5 *Composition Dimensions*

what they can do independently, and nudge their development forward. They read like writers and make books, all the while thinking about composition as much as about getting words down on paper.

All of the big ideas discussed in this chapter are connected and must be considered as part of an interrelated system. If one part of the system isn't in place and working, the system won't work. For example:

@ If children don't have an image of themselves as authors, then there isn't a need to think about making books or honoring their approximations of bookmaking. It is unlikely that they will engage in a bookmaking experience for long if they don't see making books as the kind of thing they can do or at which they can be successful.

@ If children are being pushed rather than nudged, it is likely that adults aren't comfortable with the children's approximations and are controlling too much of the writing process, resulting in students not having the opportunity to demonstrate all they are capable of doing.

@ If students aren't making books, there is little need to consider the dimensions of composition development. Most of the composition dimensions are addressed once children start to work across multiple pages.

All of these supports must be in place and work together in order to create an environment that nurtures young writers. In such an environment, writing is an enjoyable experience in which students confidently share thoughts and ideas through writing. But, what if even with this type of nurturing environment a child doesn't display much energy for writing? What if children are hesitant or reluctant to write? The rest of this book looks at ways to spark and encourage young children to write. However, strategies for sparking writing will be wasted without a supportive environment where writers can work with confidence.

Entering into Writing

If we consider these big ideas about writing, teachers can create classroom contexts that support young writers. Within this type of classroom context, one of the key questions becomes *How do we invite young children to enter into the writing process?* As teachers and parents, we invite children into writing whether we realize it or not. Some of our invitations are obvious, and some are so subtle that we may not realize that we're even sharing an invitation. But regardless of how intentional we are, children are picking up on our invitations and deciding whether writing is something they think they can do, as well as deciding if writing is something they want to do. Therefore, how we extend invitations into writing is worth considering. Throughout the rest of *Engaging Young Writers*, we will be considering possible entry points into writing for young children.

2

Entry Points into Writing for Young Children

One day early in the year I was preparing to spend the morning teaching in a preschool class. I spoke with the teacher about what she was seeing in her students' writing and what she hoped to see next. Because she was hoping to see more variety in her students' books, we decided that we wanted to open up some writing possibilities for them by using as examples several of the books they had been listening to and talking about during read-aloud that year, both books that told a story and books that taught the reader about something.

During the opening meeting we looked at a selection of books the students had already read that year and talked together about what kinds of books they were. With some support, the children were easily able to distinguish between books that told a story and books that provided information. With the children's help, we quickly sorted the books into two piles. In one pile we had storybooks like *Knuffle Bunny* (Willems 2004) and *Owl Babies* (Waddell 1992). In the other pile we had list books that were primarily nonfiction.. Next, I read *My Big Brother* (Fisher 2002)—a nonfiction list book about a baby's big brother—to the students, and we talked a bit about how this book was different from storybooks. We then had a brief discussion about the kinds of books they themselves could write: books that told a story or books that told a lot about something. Children naturally started talking about topics for their books. As they shared their topic ideas for their books, we asked them to think about whether they would write a book that would tell a story or a book that would teach someone about their topic. I wasn't expecting that they would necessarily write about the topic they were discussing during the meeting, or that they would write about it in the way they said they would. It was enough just to have a conversation about different ways they could write, which is a pretty big idea for a group of three-, four-, and five-year-olds.

During the discussion one of the students said that he was going to make a book about trains. Several students joined in and said they were going to write about trains as well. At the end of the circle time Bryan and Tom went straight to the writing center and started working on books. By the time I got there, their train books were well under way. When I asked them what kind of books they were making, they both said they were making books about trains. To clarify, I asked Bryan whether his book was more of a book that told a story or a book that told a lot about trains. He said that he was making a storybook about a train that crashes.

When looking at Bryan's book (see Figure 2.1 on page 22), you can tell that he did just what he said he was doing: writing a storybook about a train. To get the true feel for this book you'd have had to watch Bryan read it. On the second page you would have seen his finger traveling up the mountain on the right side of the page and coming down the left side with several successively louder crashes, culminating in the loud "Crash. Flat." that you see written at the bottom. You would have heard his high-pitched "screech, screech, screech" as the mechanic fixed the train on the last page. In a simple yet sophisticated way for a four-year-old, Bryan wrote a story of a train that travels up a mountain, crashes, and "gets fixed."

Meanwhile, Tom, who was also four years old, was working right next to Bryan. They worked on their books for about the same amount of time with similar amounts of energy. However, their books are very different. Tom's book is not a story, but a book that tells his reader some of what he knows about trains. When I asked Tom what type of book he was writing, he said it was a book that taught people about trains, as you can see in Figure 2.2 on page 23. You can see that he knew that different trains have different parts and different numbers of wheels. He knew that steam engines have smoke that comes out of funnels, and he knew that trains have various parts, like whistles. If you were to talk with Tom, you would find out that he knew even more about trains than what appears in his book.

What led two four-year-old children to write such different books on the same day of preschool? They both heard the same conversation during the read-aloud, and while it was designed to open up possibilities, the discussion didn't direct either of them to write a particular type of book. I suspect that even if I hadn't spoken to the class at all and had just let the kids go write, these boys would have written very different books from each other. My teaching helped open up possibilities, and it probably helped the children be a bit more articulate about their books. But I was not at all surprised by the differences in the kinds of books they wrote, regardless of my teaching points. Different students will naturally write different kinds of books. I see this frequently, not just in preschool but in kindergarten and first grade as well. Why are some children drawn to certain kinds of writing? Why do children respond differently to a variety of *entry points* into writing?

1   *A train*

The train goes up the mountain.
Then it goes down, boom, boom, boom.   **2**

3   *Crash. Flat.*

The mechanic fixes the train.
Screech, screech, screech.   **4**

FIG. 2.1   *Brian's Train Storybook*

The Concept of Entry Points

Adults naturally think and process information in different ways. For example, think about how you would give directions to someone coming to your house. Some people would use visual landmarks: turn right at the school, go past the gas station, turn left just past the big yellow house. Others would naturally use directional words: turn north, go 3.2 miles, turn east, and so on. Others would need to draw a map that gave a clear visual picture. While some people are comfortable giving or receiving any of these types of directions, some people have

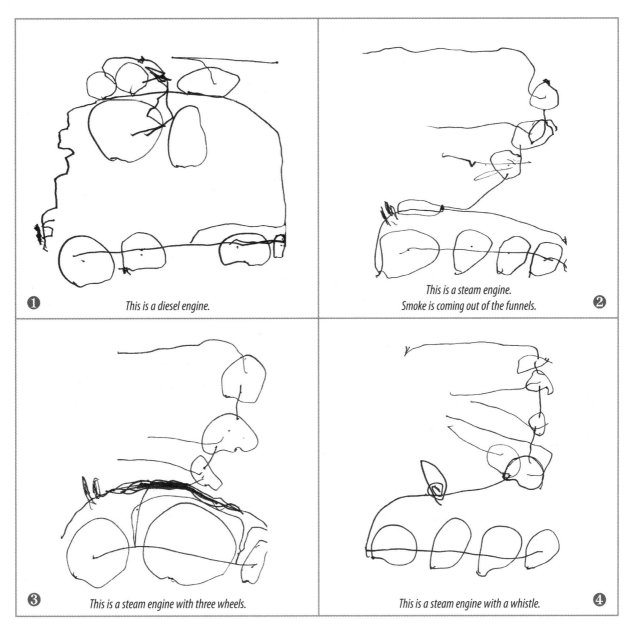

① This is a diesel engine.

② This is a steam engine.
Smoke is coming out of the funnels.

③ This is a steam engine with three wheels.

④ This is a steam engine with a whistle.

FIG. 2.2 **Tom's Train List Book**

such a natural preference that only one type of directions makes sense. These are the people who say things like, "If you want me to get there, tell me the landmarks along the way," or "Draw me a map."

You could force people to use their less preferred direction method, but it is unlikely that they would enjoy finding your house or that they would find it as easily as they would with their preferred type of directions. With continued practice they may get better at using the less preferred system, but if you want them to get to your house quickly and safely, you'll give them directions using the method that's easiest for them to understand. The hope is that your preferred direction-giving method matches their preferred direction-receiving method, or that one of you is good at translating.

Young writers aren't exactly like adult direction givers, but there are some similarities. Young writers may have a strong preference for one kind of writing over another. Some will be equally comfortable with any kind of writing. The difference of course is that as adults we don't have a vested interest in improving someone's direction-giving abilities, but as teachers we do have an interest in helping children become comfortable writing in a variety of genres.

Young children naturally think about writing books in different ways, and therefore will bring different amounts of energy to types of writing they feel more or less invested in. When I am talking about very young, inexperienced writers, I want to start with the type of writing that is most comfortable for them, the type of writing for which they have the most natural energy. Teachers should be searching for the *entry point* into the writing process that capitalizes on and maximizes each student's energy for writing. This is especially true for writers who are less confident, reluctant, or would prefer to do something other than write.

The concept of entry points into writing can be a powerful one for teachers and students. If we believe that students have different energy levels for different kinds of writing, and that providing a variety of entry points into writing will build on each student's natural inclination to write, then as teachers we should strive to find an entry point that stimulates each child's writing energy, much in the same way that we match readers to books that pique their particular interests.

Entry points are simply the angles from which we engage children in writing early on in their writing lives. Following are some potential entry points for young writers:

- *Writing about topics you know a lot about.* For some children, *nonfiction* writing about a passion or an area of expertise is more energizing than writing a narrative about an event.

- *Writing about something you have done.* Many children naturally write about personal *experiences*, so for many children, personal narrative writing is a natural entry point.

- *Writing about stories you have created.* Many children naturally tell made-up stories, whether they are oral stories or stories the kids have played during *dramatic play.*

- *Writing about favorite topics.* For many children, the energy for writing comes more from the *choice* of topic than the kind of writing, and the kind of writing will evolve naturally from that choice. For example, if a child wants to write about something that happened on the way to school, she's going to write a narrative. The next day she may want to tell you everything she knows about her dog, so she'll write a nonfiction list book about dogs.

@ *Writing for a specific purpose*. Sometimes the energy for writing comes from having a definite *reason* to make a book (or a letter, or a sign, or a list). Writing a book that will be a gift for a grandparent or making an explanatory sign for the block area might stimulate more energy than writing for other purposes.

Before moving on into an overview of the five types of entry points I review in depth in subsequent chapters, let's consider the types of writing young children tend to be drawn to.

Naming Kinds of Writing for Children

When talking with young writers, I try not to refer to either the books I read during read-aloud or the students' writing as fiction or nonfiction. There are several reasons for this. First, many of the storybooks written by children are about something they have actually done; thus, they are nonfiction. Some of their story writing is fiction and some of it is nonfiction. When teachers refer to nonfiction books, they are generally referring to books that teach people about something the author knows a lot about—books in which the author is taking an "I'm not making this up" stance. When they are asked to explain the difference between fiction and nonfiction, young children will often describe nonfiction as "true" and fiction as "made up." While this definition is essentially correct, it can be limiting. As Katie Ray wrote to me in an email on June 5, 2008, both fiction and nonfiction "are actually umbrella classifications of many different kinds of writing (genre)—classifications that in essence refer to the author's stance." As I just said, much of children's story writing may be true, but so are the books they write to tell a reader a lot about a topic. Using a nonfiction-fiction classification with young children becomes a bit confusing. Providing them with specific names for each type of writing will clarify what we mean. It is more accurate to refer to the books they write as either storybooks or list books. Storybooks can be nonfiction or fiction, while list books encompass books in which the child intends to teach readers about a topic, as well as books in which the child simply tells about a topic. Here's a brief description of each.

Storybooks. Stories can be nonfiction or fiction. Stories have story elements such as setting, characters, plot, movement through time, and change.

Stories are usually written as narratives in which something happens, then something else happens, and so on. Usually in a story there is a problem that is resolved, but the stories of many young writers are simply narrative retellings of an event.

List books. List books are usually nonfiction; they are simply books that list information about a topic. Books like "This is my mom, this is my dad, this is my brother" are list books. They list information about something—in this case, a family. Books that teach people about dogs or dinosaurs are list books as well. They list information about dogs or dinosaurs. Of course list books can quickly become more complex in their organization and the amount of information and detail they contain, but at their heart they are still list books.

Some books don't fall neatly into the storybook or list book category, but they don't fall into the fiction or nonfiction category easily either. Authors like Nicola Davies write books that contain elements of both narrative books and list books, such as *One Tiny Turtle* (Davies 2005). That's not problematic for children, and in fact, these books provide great opportunities for debate as children try to decide where these books belong in the story or list section of their classroom library.

I also generally refrain from naming the books children write *stories*, unless I am specifically referring to a story. *Story* implies narrative, and I want to be careful to use the word *story* only when I actually mean a story. When children ask to have a story read to them, they tend to expect a narrative. Therefore, if we ask children to write *stories*, we are implying that they will write narratives. That's fine, if that's what we mean to imply. But if we intend for children to have a choice about the kinds of books they are going to write, we are probably better off inviting them to write a book, using language that doesn't make any implications about whether it will be a list book or a storybook. I want to be careful not to predetermine what kind of book children will choose to write.

Children should decide what kind of book they are making. There is a useful strategy I use when I want to avoid steering a child toward writing either a storybook or a list book. When a student has just started writing a book and I'm talking with him about his book, I usually say, "What will go on the next page?" rather than "What will happen next?" The question "What happens next?" implies that the child is writing a narrative story. If the child is thinking of his book as a list book, that question is confusing. Asking, "What will go on the next page?" leaves open the possibility of the book becoming a storybook or a list book until the child decides for himself.

Avoiding the Rush to Narrative

Much of the current literature about teaching writing to young children focuses on teaching them to think and write in terms of narrative writing, whether it is personal narrative writing (writing about something a child did, using a first-person-pronoun stance) or oral storytelling. For these children, writing a story means writing a narrative. The narrative may or may not be realistic or true, but it is narrative in nature.

Children provided with this type of writing support often spend time in storytelling activities, practicing telling stories sequentially across pages. Children engage in storytelling naturally, just as they engage in dramatic play. Storytelling plays an important role in early childhood development. As Gretchen Owocki (2001) reminds us, "Valuing storytelling as you value other language events in your classroom opens doors that allow children to construct all kinds of knowledge" (102). Storytelling also "acknowledges talk as having an essential place at the core of writing" (Horn and Giacobbe 2007, 16). Oral storytelling provides a window into children's development and thinking. Storytelling definitely deserves a place in the increasingly crowded preschool, kindergarten, and first-grade day.

However, I believe that storytelling can be a parallel support for writing, not just a precursor. Some of the professional resources available today encourage children to engage in storytelling activities before they get ready to start writing. If children are already seeing themselves as writers at ages three and four in preschool, there is no need for them to stop being writers at the beginning of kindergarten so they can get ready to do something they are already comfortable with. Writing a sequentially organized narrative may not be something they are ready to do at the beginning of kindergarten, but they can certainly already put their ideas and stories on paper.

I'm not disputing the importance of narrative writing, and I also believe strongly in the importance of oral storytelling. I am simply arguing that narrative writing isn't the *only* type of writing that is appropriate for beginning writers—and that it may not be the type of writing that is most motivating for every child, nor will it be the most energizing type of writing for every child.

While narrative writing is important, it should definitely not be the only kind of writing that is privileged and valued in early childhood classrooms. Story writing is not the only possible entry point for young writers, and for some writers, story writing may actually decrease their energy for writing at a time when we want to maximize that energy.

Here are two examples of students for whom story writing was probably not the most energizing type of writing.

@ As a first grader, Adrian enjoyed making up stories at home, especially about topics related to fantasy. At school, he did not like writing workshop, perhaps for a couple of reasons: Fine motor tasks were not particularly easy for him, although his fine motor skills didn't seem to hinder him from drawing at home. Also, at school the primary type of writing he was asked to do was personal narrative—writing about something that happened to him. This type of writing simply wasn't very inviting to him. In fact, Adrian had even started writing in his own genre, fictional personal narrative. He started making up stories and passing them off as things that happened to him. One way or the other, Adrian was going to work some fantasy into his writing. Like many children, Adrian was more energized by a study of nonfiction, and since Adrian's teacher didn't require that he write about a real topic, he could incorporate his interest in fantasy by writing about dragons. His book "Dragonology" (see Figure 2.3) represented a different level of energy for writing.

@ Justin, a first grader, was not always careful during personal narrative writing, which he and his classmates had been writing for much of the year. When his class started studying nonfiction writing in April, Justin started showing a very different level of attention to his handwriting, spelling, and the overall presentation of his book. He was part of a group of children studying wolves, and he attacked his research about wolves with great energy. As he worked on his book on wolves (see Figure 2.4), his teacher noticed a higher level of attention to conventions in his writing. His spelling and spacing improved. The goal in studying nonfiction wasn't to improve Justin's spelling, although that's a nice by-product, but that was how increased energy manifested itself in Justin's writing. For Justin, nonfiction writing provided more interest, meaning, and energy to the entire writing process.

Both of these stories about young writers make me pause and wonder. What would have happened to Adrian's image of himself as a writer if he had had the opportunity to write nonfiction early in the year? What would have happened to Justin's writing if he had started writing about topics of interest, like wolves, early on in the year? My hypothesis is that Adrian and Justin, and numerous other children like them, would have benefited from entry points into writing that matched their interests and maximized their energy for writing.

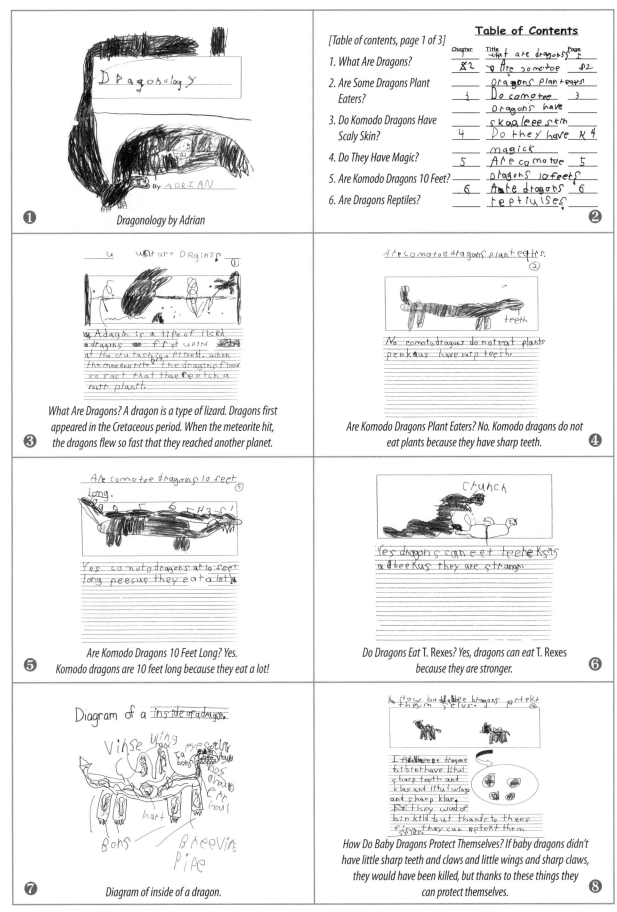

❶ *Dragonology by Adrian*

❷

❸ *What Are Dragons? A dragon is a type of lizard. Dragons first appeared in the Cretaceous period. When the meteorite hit, the dragons flew so fast that they reached another planet.*

❹ *Are Komodo Dragons Plant Eaters? No. Komodo dragons do not eat plants because they have sharp teeth.*

❺ *Are Komodo Dragons 10 Feet Long? Yes. Komodo dragons are 10 feet long because they eat a lot!*

❻ *Do Dragons Eat T. Rexes? Yes, dragons can eat T. Rexes because they are stronger.*

❼ *Diagram of inside of a dragon.*

❽ *How Do Baby Dragons Protect Themselves? If baby dragons didn't have little sharp teeth and claws and little wings and sharp claws, they would have been killed, but thanks to these things they can protect themselves.*

FIG. 2.3 **Excerpts from Adrian's Book "Dragonology"**

① The Wolf Book by Justin

② Wolves can be red. Did you know that?

③ Wolves puppies play together.
Wolves puppies howl when they are scared.

④ If you want to have a wolf as a pet you have to train it.

FIG. 2.4 *Excerpts from Justin's Book About Wolves*

The point of these stories is not to try to argue against children engaging in personal narrative writing. In fact, for some children personal narrative writing is the kind of writing they have the most energy for. For these children, writing about something they have done is the easiest kind of writing, especially if we help them see that they can write about anything they have done, big or small. If they can write about the everyday occurrences in their lives, they will never run out of topics.

Personal narrative story writing helps children sequence and organize events as they unfold through time. Writing about what they know is easier than making up a story with a beginning, middle, and end since their own experiences have these story elements built right in. Personal narrative writing is certainly a type of writing children should study. It's just not the most energizing for everyone.

Therefore, one of our goals as educators is to help young writers see the multitude of possibilities for their writing. Young children should receive energy for writing from the topics, kinds of books, and purposes they choose when they write. As children's energy and confidence grow, they will be able to tackle the variety of challenges they will face as writers.

The Importance of Talk

One way a teacher can help students find topics for writing and make decisions about the kinds of books they might make is to listen carefully to children when they are talking informally. Basically, anything that a child can talk about is something she can write about. If they can talk it, they can write it because for young children, talk is an important form of prewriting. The reverse is true as well: if a child can't talk about a potential writing topic, then it's likely that she'll have much more difficulty writing about it.

It's also important to remember that in most cases children's talk is going to be much more detailed than their writing. In fact for many authors, the challenge of writing is the attempt to narrow down talk and ideas into a written text. Very young writers will be able to talk about their topic with much more detail than is represented in their written words. Since their writing starts with talk, it is important for teachers to understand and value the importance of children's talk.

One of my favorite times to gather writing topics from preschool writers is during snack time. There's something about sitting down over food that supports conversations. During snack time there aren't as many distractions and pulls in various directions. It's a time to just talk, something that seems to be increasingly rare in our world. Invariably over snack I'll learn about areas of interest for a student, something interesting that happened last night, or plans for what he is going to do at recess today. By joining in on these conversations, I can find potential books waiting to be written.

I must say that the cafeteria isn't as much fun of a place to get writing ideas from first graders as a cozy preschool classroom at snack time is. But throughout first graders' days—in hallways, at recess, as they come into the classroom each morning—students are full of talk and stories. If teachers keep in the back of their mind that all of these stories and ideas could be potential books, they will have a wealth of ideas to offer when children are stuck with their writing. This almost sounds as if, when listening to children talk, I care only about finding book possibilities, which isn't the case. But all good teachers know their students really well. The better we know our students, their likes, interests, and issues, the better we will be able to support them as writers and the more able we will be to provide them with entry points that will energize them for writing.

Possible Entry Points for Young Writers

There are numerous entry points that may be beneficial in maximizing young children's energy for writing. In the upcoming chapters, we'll consider in depth five broad entry points into writing: essential, invitational, story, experience, and interest.

Essential Entry Points

There are several fundamental teaching concepts that can greatly influence children's motivation and energy for writing.

- *Meaning.* The more meaningful writing is to the child, the more energy he will have for writing. Helping children find meaningful things to think and write about provides a powerful pathway for entering into writing.

- *Choice.* Choice affects writing energy in many ways, from choosing a topic to choosing what kind of book to write. For many children, choice equals control, and since we want children to develop strong images of themselves as writers, we want them to have as much control over the writing process as is beneficial.

- *Purpose.* The answer to the question "Why are you writing this book?" is an important one for young children. When children have a clear, driving purpose for writing, their energy for writing increases. Teachers can help children enter into the writing process by helping them understand potential audiences for their writing.

The reason these entry points are called essential entry points is that their power is not limited to the area of writing. Meaning, choice, and purpose cut across all curricular areas. Children have more energy for math when they are solving a problem for a real purpose. Art becomes more engaging when it has true meaning for the child. Meaning, choice, and purpose are concepts that influence how learners view learning at all ages.

Invitational Entry Points

Teachers in preschool and the primary grades invite children into writing in different ways, depending on their students' developmental levels.

- In *preschool*, teachers tend to invite children to write through the *interactions* and *conversations* they have with students each day. The simple invitation to make a book may be a new one for a preschool child. Throughout the day there will be numerous opportunities to suggest that students write. Skillful teachers can begin to capitalize on opportunities that will stimulate the writing energies of each individual student.

- In *kindergarten and first grade*, teachers' writing invitations tend to present themselves within *curriculum* and *units of study*. Teachers propose that the class study a kind of writing or a part of the process of being a writer. The curriculum that results from teachers' and students' study of writing leads to an invitation to try that kind of writing themselves.

Story Entry Points

The lure of story is powerful for young children. They naturally engage in all sorts of story play, from acting out stories with action figures to participating in complex dramatic play on the playground. They quickly become dinosaurs and firemen and moms and dads. The stories that children play can be written as books and become entry points for writing.

Children sometimes incorporate characters or parts of stories they know into their play. Sometimes the characters or plots in their writing come from television and movies, but in early childhood classrooms where picture books are read and reread each day, it is just as likely that children will incorporate favorite picture book characters into their writing. Knowing some books really well through multiple read-alouds helps young children bridge the gap between their dramatic play and their book writing. As children begin to equate the stories they play with the stories they read, teachers can help them see possibilities for writing.

Experience Entry Points

For some children, writing about their lives is a natural entry point into writing. If they see that they can write about experiences from their lives, both big and small, they will always have a bank of writing topics. As children become more experienced writers, teachers can encourage them to write about experiences in more interesting ways, but for very young writers, one of the goals is simply for them to realize that they can write about experiences right from their lives.

Interest Entry Points

Most children are naturally curious observers of the world around them, and the adults in their lives can help foster that curiosity. As children learn about topics of interest they become experts on those topics. If we define experts very loosely, then all children have topics on which they are experts. We can help children enter into writing by showing them that they can share what they know about a topic with others by writing about it in a book.

The five entry points listed here certainly don't encompass all of the possible entry points for young writers. In fact, my hope is that you will find additional entry points that will make sense for the writers you nurture each day.

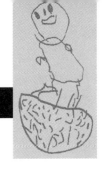

Essential Entry Points

3

▪▪▪▪▪▪▪▪▪▪▪▪▪▪▪▪▪▪▪▪▪▪▪▪▪▪▪▪▪▪▪▪▪▪▪

Meaning, Choice, and Purpose

One afternoon in May I was in the hallway at school talking to a teacher when a first-grade class walked by. Brooke, a student I've known for several years, saw me, jumped out of line, and ran over to me. She couldn't contain her desire to tell me some big news, and blurted out, "Mr. Glover, we get to name the creek!" And then just as quickly, she caught up with her class, got back in line, and headed off down the hall to recess. What led to Brooke needing to tell me something so important that she just had to get out of line and blurt it out? What led to her interest and enthusiasm for this important piece of news?

Since the beginning of the school year, Brooke's first-grade class had been studying the small creek that runs behind our school. Early in the year two of our first-grade classes had noticed that the creek did not have any water in it, which isn't unusual in late summer when it hasn't rained for a while. This led to the question "Is it a creek if it doesn't have water in it?" This question touched off a lively debate among students in the two first-grade classes (and the staff at a faculty meeting) over whether water is a necessary component of "creekness."

One idea led to another and throughout the year these classes engaged in an in-depth, long-term investigation of our creek. They created devices to measure and record the water depth and made hypotheses about where the water comes from and why it appears and disappears. When their measurement devices became stuck in the ice in the winter, they brainstormed solutions for getting them out of the ice. They interviewed a local creek expert and learned where the creek started and how it flowed to a larger creek, then to the Ohio River, and eventually to the ocean. They took a field trip to visit the origin of the creek and various locations along its journey downstream. They labeled storm water drains and put fliers in the neighborhood asking people not to dump anything in the drains since anything they dumped would end up in the creek and, eventually, the Gulf of Mexico.

Most importantly, in Brooke's opinion, her class discovered that the creek behind our school didn't have a name, so they decided to name it. They discussed numerous methods for including the entire school population in the naming process. They decided that these two first-grade classes would come up with a list of names for the rest of the students to vote on (after eliminating names like Bob). After tabulating more than nine hundred votes, they proudly announced the final choice, Discovery Creek.

Throughout this process Brooke and her classmates became deeply engaged in thinking about the creek. In looking at the story of the creek investigation that fostered this deep thinking, we can see several factors that led to Brooke needing to tell me about naming the creek. Some of these include the following:

- *Balance of control.* The teachers in these first-grade classes understood that there needs to be balance of control regarding the learning that is taking place in the classroom. These weren't teachers who just let students study whatever they wanted, nor were they teachers who totally controlled the learning, made all of the decisions in the room, and had students who were passive learners. These teachers promoted students' becoming co-controllers of the decisions, processes, and learning in the classroom. There was a balance of control between the teachers and the students.

- *Student ownership.* Over the years at our school we have become less interested in where project or investigation topics originate and much more interested in who owns the project in the end. In the end, is the investigation owned by the teachers, the students, or both? Brooke and her classmates truly owned the creek investigation, which is much more important than how it got started. Throughout the investigation, the students made key decisions about where to go next. Many of those decisions led the teachers in different directions than they originally anticipated, and sometimes teachers helped influence the direction by the questions they asked. The end result was that students understood that their opinions, ideas, and decisions were valued parts of the process.

- *Student interest.* The creek investigation became deeply engaging for students because they were truly interested in it. Regardless of what happened throughout the investigation, it is unlikely that Brooke would have displayed such enthusiasm if it had not become a topic of interest. Brooke and her classmates were generating questions for which they truly wanted answers, and for many of these questions their teachers didn't have the answers. These students developed what physicist Richard Feynman describes as "the pleasure of finding things out" (1999, 1).

@ *Time.* I am certain that Brooke would not have become deeply engaged with the study of creeks if the process had taken only a week or two. These teachers allowed students the opportunity to struggle with questions over a long period of time. Even after pondering the question for nine months, the students did not have a definitive answer as to whether it's a creek if there's no water in it (although there was a strong group of students advocating that once a creek, always a creek). That's not to say that every investigation needs to last a year. But by allowing students a long period of time to ponder questions and look for solutions, teachers provided students the opportunity to become deeply engaged.

What was perhaps most interesting about the creek study was the impact it had on students' thinking. On one of the last days of the year, one of our speech therapists was observing some students on the playground after a heavy rain. Most students were running and avoiding the puddles (or more likely finding excuses for running *into* them). There was one group of students who were bent over a large puddle, carefully studying how the light reflected off the puddle and how the ripples in the puddle would change the reflection. After eavesdropping for several minutes on their deep conversation about the puddle, the therapist entered into their conversation. The children shared their thinking and their questions. After a bit, she asked the children who their teachers were. The first graders confirmed the therapist's suspicion that they were in the classes that had been studying the creek.

At this point you might be saying to yourself, studies like the creek investigation are interesting, but what does this have to do with teaching writing? I could make an obvious connection to writing related to this investigation simply by looking at the type of writing students did within their creek investigation. Studying the creek provided numerous opportunities for authentic, purposeful writing. But we can make deeper connections between the learning related to this type of investigation and the writing experiences we hope children have in our classrooms. If we want children to become students who enjoy writing, who become deeply immersed in writing projects, who are passionate writers, then the same principles apply. If we believe that investigations of this type represent high-quality teaching and learning, then the same qualities hold true for high-quality writing instruction as well.

Essential Entry Points

The larger reason for examining in-depth, powerful learning experiences is that they present several entry points into learning, and especially into writing.

Throughout the rest of this chapter we will look at three key *essential entry points* as they relate to learning and writing: meaning, choice, and purpose. I call these essential entry points since they are based on concepts that have a powerful impact on teaching and learning. Meaning, choice, and purpose influence children's and adults' learning in any area, and they certainly affect children's desire and willingness to write.

These essential entry points are all related to the issue of motivation for writing. Yet the concept of motivation in classrooms sometimes has the connotation of getting students to do something that they might not otherwise want to do. Throughout this book we'll be looking at motivation in terms of how we create learning environments where the motivation for writing is a natural outgrowth of the classroom experiences. The goal should be for children to be intrinsically motivated to share their thinking through their writing.

Essential Entry Point: Meaning

Writing should be an enjoyable experience for all children. We should therefore be looking at other learning experiences that are enjoyable, productive, and meaningful for students when we plan our writing instruction. Unfortunately, throughout our country children are being asked to do more and more work that is of little interest and holds little meaning. Students practice reading nonsense words to hone their ability to blend sounds. They engage in math activities that are not meaningful and bear little connection to their lives. Skills are narrowed down, drilled and practiced, but with little true meaning from the perspective of a young child.

The types of experiences that we enjoy engaging in as adults are those experiences that have meaning for us, that we're interested in, and that we have an emotional response to. They're also the type of experiences that push us to think more deeply. Ellin Keene eloquently addresses this issue of emotional response in her remarkable book *To Understand: New Horizons in Reading Comprehension*:

> We know that people understand, retain, and reapply what they have learned when they have an emotional connection to it. When teachers lament the fact that children don't seem to remember and reapply what they've been taught, I worry that we have sterilized our teaching approaches and removed so much of the emotional component from our daily conversation that children have little to anchor the concepts they've been taught. (2008, 233)

Issues of meaning, interest, and emotional connection are as important for young learners as they are for adults. As we think about young learners, there are several key questions we should ask ourselves about students' learning experiences.

> How is this experience meaningful for this child? How does it relate to her life?
>
> Is the child interested in this idea, this topic, this activity?
>
> How deeply engaged is the child in this experience?

Children will stay engaged in an activity for long periods of time when the activity is interesting and engaging for them. Adults often talk of preschool children having short attention spans, and for many activities that is true. But when children engage in interesting activities of their own choosing, they will sustain their attention for long periods of time. Young children will engage in complex dramatic play and build intricate structures that require sustained concentration and attention. When children engage in an activity for a long period of time, there is the potential for deep thinking to occur.

Fostering Deep Engagement

There are several indicators of deep engagement. One indicator is the amount and quality of children's talk about a topic they are studying. How often do they initiate conversation about the topic? Brooke's talking to me in the hallway was not an unusual occurrence for her class. Children in these classes talked about the creek study frequently at school, and not just during formal creek discussions or activities. Children talk about things that interest them, so it was natural that they talked a lot about the creek.

Another indicator is whether there is evidence that children are talking at home about what they are studying in depth at school. Teachers sometimes hear parents say that they frequently get the "not much" reply when they ask their children what they did at school that day. That doesn't mean that interesting things didn't happen at school, but when students are deeply engaged, they are more likely to want to tell everyone about what they are studying, even their parents. We also see evidence of engagement when students come into school and say things like, "Last night my parents and I found a map on the Internet that shows where our creek goes," or "My dad and I figured out a new way we could measure the water in the creek." The more deeply engaged students are, the more likely they are to talk about their experiences at home.

We see further evidence of children's deep engagement when parents become engaged in the investigation as well. Several parents from the two classes studying the creek went on the field trip to figure out where the creek goes once it leaves school property. As students were asking the creek expert questions, parents started asking their own questions about the creek and building on each other's questions—evidence of their own interest in and curiosity about the creek. It should be noted that none of the parents, and probably few of the students, had a natural burning desire to learn about creeks, but when the people around you—classmates, friends, or your own children—start to think deeply about a topic you typically take for granted, you start to develop your own interest in the topic. This holds true for school principals as well, since I can now tell you exactly how many times I drive over the creek on my way home from school each day.

One final indicator of deep engagement is student behavior. It is not uncommon to see children who might be prone to misbehavior, talking when someone else is talking, or generally not paying as much attention as we would like behaving very differently when they are engaged in an activity of deep interest. It's no different for adults. Our minds tend to wander when listening to someone talk about a topic in which we have little interest. Yet when it's a topic of interest, we're on the edge of our seats, listening closely. Behavior issues decrease greatly in classrooms where students are engaged in an activity related to a deep, meaningful investigation.

Toward the end of the year I received a letter from a first-grade class that was engaged in a long-term study of recycling. In the letter the students invited me to come and talk with their class about the possibility of getting the cafeteria to stop using Styrofoam trays. I went to the classroom, eager to hear their rationale and ideas. While all of their ideas were great, there was one student whose questions and thoughts were particularly memorable. Marcus was a student whom I knew well. He had a variety of behavioral challenges that typically made it difficult for him to focus. Yet, during our cafeteria tray conversation, I felt like I was listening to a different child. While I knew that he still displayed a lot of behavior issues in school, during this conversation he was completely engaged and attentive. He listened to his classmates and shared his ideas appropriately. I later found out that he had become deeply engaged in the cafeteria tray issue, so it wasn't surprising for him to be completely focused during this conversation. During opportunities like this, teachers can see what children are capable of under optimal conditions, giving them a vision for what is possible.

Meaning, interest, and engagement alone are not enough to deem an experience valuable for a child. Children can become engaged in activities that are not particularly productive or interested in topics that may not lead to rich learning. "Engagement is not the only result one must have to ensure a quality school. The presence or absence of desired learning is—in the long run—the determining factor in assessing the quality of a school. Absent engagement, however, there is little possibility that students will learn anything the school intends for them to learn" (Schlechty 1997, 170). Our goal as educators should be to help create environments where meaningful engagement leads to authentic learning.

If the issues of meaning, engagement, and interest are vitally important for young learners, then they are certainly just as important for young writers. When we look at the amount of energy that individual children bring to the process of writing, we can rephrase the questions we asked earlier.

How is what the child is writing meaningful to him? How does it relate to his life?

How interested is the child in what he is writing about?

How deeply engaged is the child in the book he is writing?

Children must see writing as a meaningful, engaging experience. The problem with the writing experiences some children have in school is that the kinds of writing they are asked to do are kinds of writing that can be found only in schools. Teachers should be able to answer the question "Where does this type of writing occur in the world?" and if they can't (because it exists only in schools), then teachers should think about how useful this type of writing is for their students' development as writers.

I certainly understand that every single piece of writing a child produces will not necessarily be the result of deep engagement and interest. I also understand that there may be times that children will engage in writing that is not reflective of real-world writing, such as on standardized tests. However, at the very least, teachers should carefully look at a balance over the course of a year.

Essential Entry Point: Choice

The role of choice is another major factor in creating effective learning experiences for young children. If we look at a typical student day and analyze how many true choices a student has each day, we see that in many classrooms children are presented with few options. Yet as educators we know that choice plays a major role in learning.

When a child has a choice, he has some degree of control over the learning experience. This is particularly important for children who feel that the world of school is stacked against them or children who have little control in their lives outside of school. Children, as well as adults, need to have what Peter Johnston calls a sense of agency, a feeling "that if they act, and act strategically, they can accomplish their goals" (2004, 29). Agency gives children the knowledge that their actions have an impact on the world around them, as well as their own lives, and that their actions are important. Choice is one of the ways that children can develop a sense of control over their world.

This doesn't mean that just having choices is enough. As Tom Newkirk reminds us, "We cannot speak for long about choice without having to modify it—it is not simply choice that we are after, but wise choice or intelligent choice" (1989, 184). With the classroom environment, the teacher sets up boundaries for choices and certainly discourages some choices. Yet within a nurturing classroom environment there are numerous opportunities for all children to make choices and decisions that affect their learning, both as individual learners and as a class of learners.

While children are learning to think, to compose, to write, there should be as much choice provided as possible. The stance teachers take on choice is a major factor in supporting children as writers. "Student choice is the crucial fuel that drives a healthy workshop" (Fletcher and Portalupi 2001, 23). Within the context of writing, there are numerous potential choices that can increase children's energy for writing. The actions of teachers determine which choices exist in a classroom.

The following are some of the potential choices young children have when writing.

Choice of When to Write

In kindergarten and first-grade classrooms, children are writing during writing workshop and, we hope, at other times during the day. In preschool, however, it is more developmentally appropriate for children to choose when to write themselves. On any given day, a preschool child may choose to write or not to write. I expect that all preschool children will choose to write at various times throughout the year. Much of this book discusses strategies for supporting children in making the decision to write.

Choice of Topic

Topic choice is perhaps the most important source of energy for writing. If teachers choose what a child will write about, they are assuming that the child "is not capable of choosing his own topics for writing, or that he would have little interest in choosing them—that what he's writing about wouldn't matter that much to him" (Ray and Glover 2008, 9). If we pick a topic for a child, we are assuming that she would be just as happy writing about the given topic as she would be writing about one she had picked on her own. While there are some children who will write about any assigned topic, most children will bring greater energy to writing when they are writing about something they care about. This makes sense for writers of all ages.

Think about how many choices adults make in their lives. We decide what books to read and movies to watch based on our interests. If we want children to become passionate about their writing, then allowing (and encouraging) them to choose topics that matter becomes crucial. We should also teach students to develop the *ability* to choose topics for themselves. While there will be times later in school when children must write on certain topics, we don't want children to become reliant on someone else to provide them with a topic. Strategies for supporting children's abilities to choose a topic are discussed in Chapter 4.

Choice of Genre

As discussed in Chapter 2, children will have greater energy for different kinds of writing. Some children will naturally gravitate toward story writing while other children will naturally want to write nonfiction list books. Within genre studies in kindergarten and first grade, children will be attempting writing in particular genres, but there should also be times throughout the year when they are choosing their own genres. One of our goals as teachers of young writers should be to help them learn to match genre choice with their purpose for writing.

Choice of Length

Another important goal for young writers is learning to decide when their writing is finished. The answer to "How do you know your book is finished?" shouldn't be "Because I've filled the pages." We want children to think critically about how and when a book is finished.

One of the potential dangers in giving young writers books that are prestapled, which I do recommend for preschool and kindergarten, is that this format might communicate to young writers how long a book should be. Therefore, early on we should show children that they can add to their books by stapling on more pages or shorten their books by simply removing pages. Children quickly become comfortable with this process and then have the ability to determine the length of their own writing.

Choice of Paper

With preschool writers I generally use blank paper books, which provide limitless choices for placement of pictures and words on a page. With kindergarten and first grade, the number of lines on a page starts to communicate how much writing should go on a page. Since I want children making as many wise choices as possible, I want children to have a variety of paper options so they can choose paper that fits their purpose for writing.

All of these choices and others shift the balance of control from teacher to students. That's not to say that teachers are giving up all control or taking a passive stance in the classroom. But teachers who are helping children learn to make choices show that they understand the energy that choice brings to writing.

Essential Entry Point: Purpose

Learning should have meaning for students. It should be interesting and engaging. But when teachers help students find genuine purposes for learning, we raise the bar even higher. When students have a genuine purpose for learning, their energy and passion will increase.

Children ultimately control what is learned. According to Loris Malaguzzi, the founder of the early childhood schools in Reggio Emilia, Italy, "What children learn does not follow as an automatic result from what is taught. Rather, it is in large part due to the children's own doing as a consequence of their activities and our resources" (Edwards, Gandini, and Forman 1998, 67). Ralph Fletcher and JoAnn Portalupi (2001) build on this thought by saying, "While the teachers may determine what gets taught, only the student can decide what will be learned. This is true for learners of any age. We learn best when we have a reason that propels us to want to learn" (9). How often do our students have a reason that propels their learning? Understandably, every classroom experience can't produce deeply purposeful learning filled with passion. But a child's school life shouldn't be void of meaningful purpose either.

Just as we see changes in students when they are engaged in purposeful learning, we see changes in student writing when they are writing for a real purpose. "When students have an authentic purpose for their writing—whether to document an important event in their lives, get classmates to laugh, or communicate a message that matters—they pay attention differently to instruction. Our students know best which topics and purposes for writing matter most to each of them. Letting them choose their own topics and set their own purposes makes it more likely they'll be engaged and receptive" (Fletcher and Portalupi 2001, 10). As teachers of writing we should be asking ourselves, "Why do my students want to write each day?" Our hope should be that they are writing for real purposes, not just writing because it is time for writing workshop.

Several years ago I had the pleasure of watching literacy expert Shelley Harwayne work with a group of first graders during a demonstration lesson. The children were sitting at a table and were working on various writing projects. Shelley was conferring with them about their writing and providing constructive feedback to help them think more deeply about their work. As Shelley was talking with one girl, she asked her this simple but critical question:

"Where will your book be when it's finished?"

The girl looked puzzled and paused for a moment while Shelley patiently waited for a reply. Finally the girl said, "I guess it will be at home somewhere."

This is a pretty typical response for many first graders. They're simply doing what they're doing because it's expected of them, without a real plan for how each piece will go out into the world when it's finished. They're writing in writing workshops either because they truly enjoy writing or because it's expected that they'll be writing. While we want students to be writing because they enjoy it, we also want students to be writing with a real purpose in mind.

We should want more for our students. We can help them to write with a particular, purposeful aim and thus to be able to reply with a greater sense of purpose when we ask where their writing will be in two weeks, perhaps with answers like these:

- ℮ I'm going to give this book to my grandpa. It's about the time we went fishing together and I'm going to give it to him as a gift.

- ℮ I'm writing a book about how to eat lunch in the cafeteria. I'm going to give it to my teacher so she can read it to her students at the start of next year so they can learn the cafeteria rules.

- ℮ I'm writing a book that teaches people a lot about horses. I'm going to put it in our class library along with the other animal books.

- ℮ I'm writing a book about my first day of school because it's a day I want to remember.

Thinking about purposes for writing helped me in a writing conference I had with Julia, an extremely deep-thinking first grader. As I sat down next to Julia I asked her what she was writing about. She said that she was writing a book about her favorite series of books. I soon learned that she loved Junie B. Jones books and had read most of the ones in a book bin in her class. She was working on a book about Junie B. Jones books. Each page was almost a mini book review of a book she had read.

When I asked Julia about where her book would be in a couple of weeks, she said she wasn't sure. We talked for a moment about how her book might help other children in her class. We imagined that perhaps one of her classmates thought she might try out a Junie B. Jones book but wasn't sure which one to read first. Julia thought that her book might help other children decide which books they might like and I suggested that perhaps it could stay in the bin with all of the Junie B. Jones books. Julia liked the idea and continued working on her book, now with a clear purpose for her book in mind and an idea for where it might be in two weeks. Regardless of whether her book ended up in the Junie B. Jones bin for the rest of the year or not, this conversation hopefully helped Julia, and her classmates who were at the table listening in, understand that the students' books could serve a purpose in their classroom.

When children write with a purpose, they are writing with the thought that they are writing for someone. They're writing with an audience in mind. Often they are writing for themselves, but children can learn to write for other audiences as well. When children think that someone will actually read their writing, they think differently about the message they are communicating.

Elizabeth was in kindergarten when she wrote a book about going to her friend Megan's house. As she reread her book to her kindergarten teacher, she realized that someone reading her book might be confused at a couple of points. At first her book didn't say that Megan was her friend. Elizabeth said, "I knew my reader would be confused and wonder, 'Who is Megan?' so I added this part about Megan being my friend. And then at this part where Megan and I did Pilates, I had to go back and add in that we did Pilates with our moms. I didn't want my reader to think, 'What, you just went upstairs and turned on the TV and started doing Pilates?' So I added in the part about doing Pilates with the moms." (See Figure 3.1.)

I didn't want my readers to be confused. Isn't that what writers should be saying to themselves all the time? Twice in this short kindergarten book, Elizabeth's thinking about her readers led her to make revisions by adding to her story to clarify meaning.

How often do children think about their readers when they are writing? In order to think about their readers, children must actually have readers for their books. There are numerous opportunities for children to have audiences for their books, including these:

- At the end of a unit of study in kindergarten or first grade, the class can have a formal writing celebration where students publish books written during that unit to share with others.

- In the middle of a unit of study, the class can have less formal celebrations when children simply have a chance to read their writing to a classmate.

- In addition to being a teaching time, the share time portion of writing workshop provides an opportunity for children to share and talk about their books.

- At any point in their writing students can stop and read their books to other students in the room. In preschool classrooms it's fairly easy to ask a child to read a newly finished book to another student in the room, and preschoolers are usually eager audiences. In kindergarten and first grade students can have more established writing partners whom they can read their books to and get feedback from on their writing. Even more motivating for some children is the opportunity to read their book to a student in another class or grade.

- For many young children, getting to read their book to an adult in the room or school is especially meaningful. In preschool classes there are often other adults present to read to. In kindergarten and first-grade classes a secretary, the previous year's teacher, or the art teacher can provide a

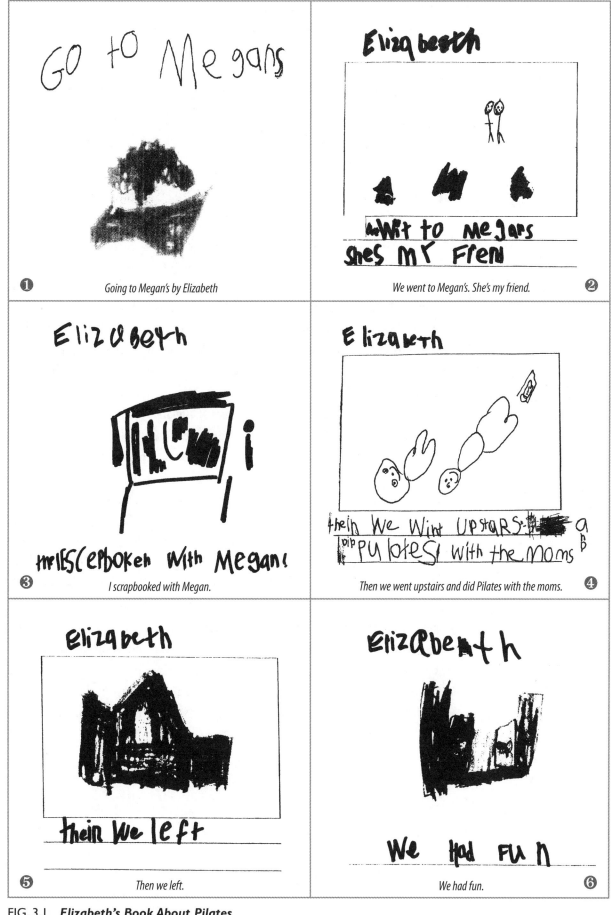

1 Go to Megans

Going to Megan's by Elizabeth

2 Elizqbeth

Wit to Megans Shes my Fren

We went to Megan's. She's my friend.

3 Elizabeth

theISCepboken With Megan!

I scrapbooked with Megan.

4 Elizabeth

thein We Wint UPStaRS

Did PU lotes! with the moms

Then we went upstairs and did Pilates with the moms.

5 Elizabeth

their We left

Then we left.

6 Elizabeth

We Had FUn

We had fun.

FIG. 3.1 **Elizabeth's Book About Pilates**

particularly special audience. Adults also provide good audiences since they are likely to ask good questions and share specific comments about a child's writing.

However we do it, we want to be sure young children have plenty of readers. When they are writing with readers in mind, children move beyond writing just to write or because we ask them to.

Not as Hard as It Seems

Trying to make every moment in a classroom deeply engaging for each and every child can start to feel overwhelming. When teachers have a clear vision for the best possible learning experiences and environment, it is easy to become discouraged when the gap between the reality and what is desired seems to be too large. By focusing on the entry points of meaning, choice, and purpose both in learning in general and in writing specifically, and by working to nudge (not push) our own development as educators, we can nurture memorable learning for children.

Several years ago the *Hundred Languages of Children* exhibit was in a museum in Columbus, Ohio. My sister, a preschool speech pathologist, and her then thirteen-year-old son, Patrick, were visiting the museum and stopped in briefly to see the exhibit. The *Hundred Languages* exhibit shares images and text of students' learning experiences from the amazing early childhood programs in Reggio Emilia, Italy. It's the type of exhibit you could spend ten minutes walking through or spend days thinking about its meaning. Patrick, being thirteen, was on the shorter end of that spectrum. After looking at the exhibit and asking his mom some questions, he tried to make sense of it with the following statement: "So this whole thing basically says that you'll learn more if you learn about something you care about? Don't adults already know that?" In one quick teenage summation, Patrick stated what teachers know but sometimes forget. If we can keep in the front of our minds the roles of meaning, choice, and purpose in our teaching, our students will surprise us with the depth of their thinking. And, if we think of meaning, choice, and purpose as entry points for writing, we will help our students care deeply about their writing.

Invitational Entry Points

■■■ ■■■ ■■■ ■■■ ■■■ ■■■ ■■■ ■■■ ■■■ ■■■ ■■■ ■■■ ■■■

Conversations and Curriculum

As teachers, we extend invitations to learn each day in our classrooms. While we certainly have expectations of our students, when we think about involving children in the learning process, invitations provide a sense of mutual coming together to learn. After all, we all like to be invited to do things. The difference in school is that we don't really make declining an invitation an option.

When we look specifically at writing, there are some differences between how we invite preschool children and how we invite primary-grade children to enter into the writing process. But before we look at how the invitations are different, we must first clearly understand how bookmaking and writing are similar and different in preschool and in the primary grades. Then, considering these differences, we'll look at ways we can invite young children to write.

A Comparison of Writing in Preschool and in Grades K and 1

When looking at children's writing that comes from kindergarten and first-grade students who are engaged in effective writing workshops, it can be tempting to think that we can simply transplant a primary-grade writing workshop structure into preschool. But there are significant developmental differences between preschool and primary-grade writers that require different structures for each group. There are more appropriate ways of supporting preschool writers than simply using a K–1 writing workshop model.

Part of what makes thinking about appropriate structures for different ages tricky is that the underlying concepts are the same in preschool as they are in kindergarten and first grade. In fact, most of the big ideas for writing that are described in Chapter 1 are basically the same for writers of any age. For example:

- *Honoring approximations.* Anytime someone is trying something new as a writer, teachers must honor the child's approximation of what he is trying to do. This is the same for the seventh grader who is writing a commentary for the first time, as it is for the fourth grader who is writing a travel article for the first time, as it is for the preschooler who is writing a book for the first time. Each child is going to do it like a child of that age trying it for the first time, because he *is* a child of that age trying it for the first time.

- *Reading like a writer.* Writers of all ages study what more experienced authors do in their writing and then try it out in their own writing. Whether it's a three-year-old noticing that books have pictures and words or a sixth grader noticing that many essays don't reveal their thesis in the first sentence, the student is noticing and then trying new ideas or techniques out for herself.

- *Image of self as a writer.* If children at any age do not see themselves as writers, they will have a difficult time putting forth the effort to write and write well. While there are reluctant preschool writers, it is relatively easy to help young children see themselves as writers. There are probably many more seventh graders than three-year-olds who don't think of themselves as writers.

- *Importance of vision.* At any age children should have a clear vision for what they are trying to make as a writer. Thirteen-year-olds should be able to answer the question "What are you reading that is like what you are trying to write?" as easily as a five-year-old might answer the same question (Ray 2006).

These ideas and others cut across age groups. Certainly, a three-year-old reading like a writer will look very different from a first grader reading like a writer, but the underlying habit of mind is the same. However, the structures in preschool and the primary grades are different.

Structure: Similarities and Differences

In terms of the structures that support writing in preschool and in the primary grades, there are more similarities than differences, especially if we look at the big picture. In both preschool and K–1, the structure at its broadest level unfolds in basically same way, namely: whole-group teaching, one-on-one and small-group teaching, and whole-group sharing.

Daily Structure: Whole-Group Teaching— Read-Alouds and Minilessons

In preschool, whole-group teaching takes place within the context of a read-aloud, during which time the teacher and students are noticing what an author did in a book and thinking about how they might try this out in their own books. Sometimes the teacher is doing the noticing and sometimes, especially later in the year, the observations about authors' and illustrators' decisions are coming from students. The teaching point is embedded naturally in the read-aloud, so it's not really a minilesson.

For example, early in the year in a preschool class, students were just starting to notice the intentional decisions authors and illustrators make in their books. I wanted to make sure that children realized that a real person actually made these books and decided what the words and pictures would be. We had read several books by Donald Crews in an effort to build his identity as a person who makes books. On the day I read *Freight Train* (1985), I embedded several questions and statements about the decisions Donald had made, such as these:

Do you think the train is going slow or fast on this page? How can you tell? How did Donald draw this so that it would look like it was going fast?

Look at how smart Donald is. He wanted to show that it was night so he made this page almost all black.

Throughout the reading of the book, I referred to Donald as if he were just another person in the room. Through repeated references to Donald over several books, children began to realize that Donald made numerous decisions in order to make his books just the way he wanted them.

In kindergarten and first-grade classrooms that have writing workshops, writing time usually begins with a whole-group minilesson focused on a specific, teacher-selected teaching point. This might be presented as a directed five- to eight-minute teaching time or a longer, more flexible teaching time when the subject of the minilesson is more inquiry based. In a K–1 minilesson the teaching point is more explicit than in preschool. It is frequently connected to a book that has been read aloud and to noticing what an author has done. The minilesson could also be built around noticing the smart decisions a student in the class has made as an author in her own writing.

Individual and Small-Group Teaching: Side-by-Side Teaching and Conferring

The individual and small-group time looks very similar in preschool and K–1 classes. In preschool, side-by-side teaching occurs when students are choosing to write during choice time and the teacher is sitting down next to a child, talking about his book and choosing something to teach him about being a writer. The teacher isn't trying to fit in as many writing conferences as possible, as she may do during K–1 writing time, but she does need to monitor and support the other things students are doing during this time.

In K–1 classrooms all children are writing during writing workshop. When students are working independently, the teacher is conferring with individual students or small groups of students about writing. When a teacher is conferring one-on-one with a student, she is talking with a student about her writing and selecting something to teach her about writing. Since all of the students are writing at the same time, it is a bit easier for the teacher to follow a schedule and ensure she meets with all students on an individually appropriate basis.

The basic conference is the same in preschool and in grades K and 1, but the structure during which it occurs is different: choice time versus writing workshop.

Whole-Group Teaching: Share Time

Both preschool and K–1 writers benefit from a share time. This share time is a second valuable whole-group teaching time that comes from that day's student writing. The teacher highlights smart decisions that children made in their writing that day and helps other children envision trying out those ideas in their writing.

There are a few differences between share time in preschool and in primary-grade writing workshops. One difference is when this share time occurs. In preschool, it happens at some point later in the day after children have been writing. It might come at the end of choice time when the class is talking about what types of things children worked on that day. It might come later in the day at a closing circle time. In kindergarten and first-grade classrooms the share time comes at the end of writing workshop. Another difference between the two types of share times is that in preschool students might be sharing many things they did during their day, while in the primary grades the sharing is more tightly focused on what just occurred in writing workshop. Finally, in preschool classrooms the connection back to the teaching point that was made during the read-aloud is fairly subtle. In the primary grades the connection back to the minilesson's teaching point is more explicit. Simply put, teachers tend to be more explicit and direct as children get older and more receptive to direct explanations.

Yearly Structure: Focus Ideas and Units of Study

In preschool, teachers focus on an idea over time in the context of books read aloud. For example, over the course of several weeks in a preschool classroom, we may decide to read nonfiction books and talk about how authors sometimes write about topics that they know a lot about and want to teach to others. Here are some other possible focus ideas for preschool students (Ray and Glover 2008):

- People write books and you can, too.

- People write about many different things.

- Authors and illustrators make decisions about their books.

- Books have pictures and words (strategies for adding writing).

- Authors sometimes write about something they did (personal narrative).

- Authors sometimes write about something they know a lot about (nonfiction).

Kindergarten and first-grade writing workshops are organized into units of study. There are two basic types of units of study: product studies and process studies (Ray and Cleaveland 2004, 105). Product studies focus on studying how a text is written—including studying genre, punctuation, structure, and craft. Within process studies, children study the processes authors use. For example, a study of where authors get ideas for writing is a study of a writer's process (Ray and Cleaveland 2004, 105).

Focus ideas in preschool and units of study in primary writing workshops are similar in terms of content. In both preschool and K–1 classrooms, we look at how books are written, where writers get ideas, and how writers write when they want to teach someone about a topic, for example. The difference comes in when we examine the structures and expectations of preschool and K–1 writing time. In preschool the teaching is subtly embedded in the context of read-alouds and conversations, and different children may be writing in many different ways. We're not expecting that all preschoolers will produce a piece, for example, of nonfiction writing. In K–1, however, if we have spent several weeks studying nonfiction, we certainly expect that children will try to do some nonfiction writing.

Other Key Differences

There are other key differences between writing in preschool and writing in kindergarten and first grade.

When to Write

In Preschool

Preschool children choose when and if they write. While I expect all children to choose to write on a regular basis throughout the year (usually once or twice a month, although some children choose to write much more frequently), on any given day children in preschool will be choosing whether to write or not. All children are not expected to write on the same day at the same time.

In K–1 Classes

Grades K–1 children are writing in a writing workshop. In a writing workshop all children are writing at the same time. In whole-day classrooms students generally have writing workshop each day. In half-day kindergarten classes like we have in my district, classes generally have writing workshop three or four days a week.

How Long to Write

In Preschool

Children write for as long as their interest is sustained in preschool. They might write for five minutes or much longer. I've often been surprised by preschoolers who will become totally absorbed in a book they are working on and write for thirty minutes or more—just like how they get absorbed in building with blocks or other activities. The key is that the children themselves determine how long they will write.

In K–1 Classes

Children in grades K and 1 are working on writing for the entire time during the independent writing portion of writing workshop. This time may increase over the course of the year as children build stamina for writing. The teacher determines how long children will write. When a child finishes a book, he can choose to add to his book or he can start a new one. Children also may spend time thinking, planning, or talking about their books, but during writing workshop they are each working in some way on writing.

In preschool and kindergarten the basic concepts are the same, and the broad, overall teaching structures are somewhat similar. The differences come in the structure of writing in preschool and kindergarten classrooms. The chart in Figure 4.1 summarizes the similarities and differences between preschool and the primary grades.

Support Structures in Preschool and Primary Grades	
Structural Similarities	
Preschool	**K–1**
Read-Aloud • reading like a writer • envisioning writing • published books, student books, my books • book/topic choice	*Minilesson* • reading like a writer • envisioning writing • published books, student books, my books • book/topic choice
Side-by-Side Teaching • importance of making books—vision • topic choice—energy and quality • always teaching—nudging versus pushing • what can a child do independently and with a bit of adult support • teaching of strategies	*Conferring* • importance of making books—vision • topic choice—energy and quality • always teaching—nudging versus pushing • what can a child do independently and with a bit of adult support • teaching of strategies
Share Time • audience, readers for children's books • teaching—pointing out smart things children did in their books that day and envisioning for others	*Share Time* • audience, readers for children's books • teaching—pointing out smart things children did in their books that day and envisioning for others
Structural Differences	
Preschool	**K–1**
Children choose when to write.	Children write in writing workshop.
Most children are not writing every day.	All children write on a regular weekly schedule.
Children aren't all writing at the same time.	Children are writing at the same time.
Strategies appropriate for preschool.	Strategies appropriate for kindergarten and grade 1.
Organized by focus ideas.	Organized by units of study.

FIG. 4.1 *Structure of Writing: Similarities and Differences Between Preschool and Grades K–1*

Invitational Entry Points for Reluctant Writers

Now that we know the similarities and differences between writing structures in preschool and the primary grades, let's turn our attention to how teachers invite children at each stage into writing in each setting.

How teachers invite children into writing is particularly important for children who are less eager to write. In both preschool and primary classrooms there will be children for whom writing is less easy, who are reluctant to write. The term *reluctant writer* is often used for children who don't enjoy writing or are less eager to write. However, the term *reluctant writer* has a different meaning in preschool than in kindergarten and first grade.

In preschool, since children are choosing when to write, a reluctant writer is simply a child who is not choosing to write on a regular basis. For these children the challenge becomes helping them make the decision to write in as natural a way as possible.

In the primary grades, reluctant writers may present themselves in a variety of ways. They can be children who already have a weak image of themselves as writers and may not believe that they can write or who do not think they are good at writing. They might be children who can't find a writing topic and who do everything they can to put off writing. They simply don't enjoy writing. Since there is a portion of the day when they are required to write, the challenge for teachers becomes helping these children see writing in a more positive light.

For both types of reluctant writers, entry points into writing become especially important. That's not to say that entry points aren't important for those preschoolers who choose to write each day or the kindergarten and first graders who moan when writing workshop comes to an end. Effective entry points help provide energy and motivation for enthusiastic writers as well. Regardless of whether we're talking about reluctant or avid writers, how we invite children to write will influence their growth as writers.

Invitational Entry Points in Preschool: Conversations and Interactions

When I'm speaking with preschool teachers one of the questions that often comes up is "What about students who do not regularly choose to write?" The ideas shared throughout this book help answer this question in deeper ways, but there are also some quick and easy methods we can use to invite children into the writing process.

The following questions are simple ways of inviting children to write.

- "What are you going to write about today?" With this question we make the assumption that the child was already planning to make a book today, which might be all it takes to encourage her to actually make one.

- "Were you thinking of making a book today?" A child's response is often "Yeah, I was going to make a book today," even though he had probably not thought of it until right then.

- "If you decide to make a book today, let me know so I can watch you write."

- "I haven't seen you make a book in a while. Are you going to make one today?"

- "What is your next book going to be about?" I ask this question frequently, partially because it just assumes that students will keep making books. I often ask this when a child finishes a book, or at any point during the day since I want to encourage children to be thinking of book topics throughout the day.

- "If you were going to make a book about that, what would you put on the first page?"

For most preschool writers these invitations are all it takes to provide the spark needed to decide to write. There are some preschool writers, however, for whom these gentle nudging invitations aren't enough. The entry points discussed in Chapters 3, 5, 6, and 7 provide meaningful ways to engage these reluctant writers in writing experiences.

There is an even smaller number of children who are more openly reluctant writers. With most children, if my goal were simply to *get* them to write, I could. If compliance is my only goal, I can generally get that, although the writing usually isn't very good and the child generally doesn't enjoy the process. For young writers, the act of initiation is particularly important. "Someone who initiates an act of writing, and particularly a person who initiates an act of writing like making a book, possesses both the desire and belief that he or she is capable of writing a book. What's important for teachers to understand is how critical it is to support both dispositions—desire and belief—because they form the very core of the child's image of himself or herself as a capable writer" (Ray and Glover 2008, 90). At this point, after lots of practice, I very rarely see students who don't choose to write over time.

It's also important with preschoolers to remember that they are not expected to write every day. It's not a big deal if on any given day a child decides not to write. Instead, as Katie Ray and I discussed via email on June 5, 2008, I'm looking for patterns of reluctance to write that appear over a period of time that "might hint that the child is thinking 'I can't do that so I'm not going to choose to do it'."

Nudging Toward Writing

When I first start talking with a preschool child who seems to be resisting choosing to write, initially I'm not even trying to get him write a book. Rather, I'm laying a foundation for future writing by talking with him about something he might be able to write about at another time. It often sounds like the following interaction with four-year-old Alex.

Several months into the school year, I knew that Alex had still not chosen to make a book. After watching Alex for a while as he played in several areas of the classroom, I went over and sat down next to him and started talking. I didn't have a blank book or markers anywhere near me.

Matt: Were you thinking of making a book today, Alex?

Alex: No.

Matt: I noticed that you have been playing with some toy animals in the block area. What animal were you?

Alex: I was the cheetah. Did you know that cheetahs are really fast?

Matt: Really? How do you know that?

Alex: I know a lot about cheetahs.

Matt: What else do you know about cheetahs?

Alex actually knew quite a bit about cheetahs and easily shared what he knew. At this point Alex and I were just talking about cheetahs, much like a teacher and a student might talk about any topic of interest.

After several minutes of cheetah chat, I asked Alex if he had ever thought about writing a book about cheetahs since he knew so much about them.

Alex: Maybe tomorrow.

Matt: You know, I won't be here tomorrow. I'd love to watch you write that book. Do you think you might do it today?

Alex: No, I think I'll do it tomorrow.

Now I could certainly have gotten Alex to write this book right then if I had wanted to force the issue, but I would have run the risk both of it being more my book than Alex's and of getting him into a writing experience for which he had very little energy. So I let it go. I also could have ended the conversation there. If I had, the interaction would have been valuable on its own since it had helped Alex think about a topic for a book he might write. But Alex kept talking about cheetahs and seemed to be enjoying the interaction, so I kept talking too.

After a few more minutes, I said, "Alex, I'm excited to come back next week to see the book you're going to write about cheetahs tomorrow. I was wondering, of all of the things you know about cheetahs, which thing do you think you'll put on your first page?" Again, I didn't have a blank book or markers even nearby. We were just talking about the ideas for a book.

Matt: So, what do you think will go on the first page?

Alex: I think I'll show a cheetah going really fast.

Matt: Wow, what colors will you use?

Alex: Orange and black.

Matt: And are you going to make the cheetah big or small?

Alex: Pretty big.

Matt: Alex, could you show me how big? Would you go over to the writing center and get a blank book?

Alex: I'm not going to make it today.

Matt: I know, I'd just like to think about how you're going to do this on the first page.

Alex: OK. [*Alex happily went to get a blank book.*]

Matt: All right, Alex. Can you show me where you would put the cheetah on this page?

Alex: Sure, it will go right here.

Matt: Are you going to put a tail on the cheetah?

At this point Alex gave me the look I frequently get from children—the "Wow, I thought adults were supposed to be smart" look. Alex said, "Of course I'm going to put a tail. They're really long."

We talked for a bit about how he'd draw the cheetah and what else would go on the first page. I then asked him what would go on the second page and so on. Alex planned out what would go on each page. Again, we didn't have any markers or crayons nearby. We were just talking about possibilities.

At this point I could have asked again if he wanted to do it today. If I had and he had said no, I would have been fine with that. We actually just had a really nice conversation about writing. It was such a nice conversation that I didn't want to risk ruining by asking once more. But I didn't have to, because when we got to the fourth page, I said, "Is the mom cheetah on this page going to be bigger than the baby cheetah?"

Alex replied, "Let me show you." He went over to the writing center and got a marker. We sat at a table and he started drawing the picture for this page pretty easily. He then proceeded without prompting to work on several other pages in his book.

I knew that Alex was reluctant to choose to write, and initially when I asked him if he wanted to write, he was pretty adamant in replying no. But I also believe that after talking about his book (which he did eagerly) the whole process seemed much more attainable for him. When providing an attainable vision was coupled with honoring and celebrating what Alex put on the page, his attitude changed. Again, I could have gotten compliance if I had wanted. But what I wanted was the energy for writing to come from Alex, and it did.

I wish I could report that Alex went on to write a book every day during choice time and that overnight he became the most enthusiastic writer in his class. That would be too much to hope for from one brief interaction. But Alex's attitude about writing did seem to change and he started choosing to write on his own more often. For Alex, getting over the initial hump of writing and building the memory that he could write was all he needed.

For other students, this process might take place across several days or several weeks, comprising gentle nudging and pulling back when needed. But with this kind of support being provided over time, I rarely have a child who doesn't eventually choose to write. And as Alex knows (and my four-year-old daughters remind me daily), I'm not all that smart, so if I can do this, anyone can.

Finally, it's important to state that I've seen this kind of interaction play out with children regardless of gender, age, race, or socioeconomic level. While our school isn't as diverse as the school you may work in, we do have a range of diversity. Half of our preschool students have disabilities, many of them quite involved. Our preschool students run the developmental range from six months to six years—quite a wide spectrum of development. I simply have not seen any difference among different types of children in their willingness to make books when the right classroom conditions are in place.

If Alex had written this book the next day, I also wouldn't have been the least bit concerned if it was a totally different book than the one we had talked about, or if it had been a story about a cheetah rather than a book listing all sorts of things he knew about cheetahs. This happens frequently with preschool students and is developmentally appropriate, so it wouldn't concern me. My goal was for him to write and see himself as capable of writing, so I would have been thrilled with any writing on any topic at that point in time.

Since preschoolers are choosing if and when to write, I actually see very few preschool children who look like primary-grade reluctant writers: children who sit down to write and become stuck. Since they've already initiated the writing process, preschoolers generally have something to write about.

At some point early in most children's lives, they weren't reluctant to write. At some point, perhaps when they were toddlers, if children were given a marker and paper, they did something with them and showed an adult proudly what they had accomplished. Since most children were very young, adults responded positively to those first scribbles on paper, and their images of themselves as writers were strengthened. Unfortunately some children lose this image over the years. This happens at least in part because some adults don't see children as capable of writing and don't provide them with the appropriate nurturing supports that strengthen their images of themselves as writers. Our job as educators should be to ensure that all children see themselves as capable of doing great things.

Invitational Entry Points in Grades K–1: Possible Beginning-of-the-Year Units of Study

One of the goals for teachers early in the year is to capitalize on individual student energy and motivation for various types of writing. Since we believe that students will have different levels of energy for different types of writing, we want writers in kindergarten and first grade to engage in the type of writing for which they have the most energy. If we jump right into one particular type of writing with students, we run the risk of making writing less enticing for children than it could be.

If teachers want to capitalize on student energy right from the start of the year in kindergarten and first grade, then they should think carefully about the early units of study they are selecting to invite students to enter into writing. Some possible units to start the year are

- Launching Writing Workshop: Logistics, Routines, and Procedures

- Where Writers Get Ideas

- Using Drawing to Convey Meaning

- Genre Overview: What Types of Books Might We Make This Year?

- Reading Like a Writer

Before looking at each of these units, there are several points to consider. These units are process studies rather than product studies. The advantage of starting with a process unit is that it allows students to write in the genre of their choice. I'm also not suggesting that teachers would necessarily choose to engage students in each of these units of study. They are intended to give teachers some options from which to choose. Finally, in-depth information about each of these units can be found in various resources. Here, we will focus on considering the units next to each other in the context of providing energy for young writers.

Launching Writing Workshop: Logistics, Routines, and Procedures

There is certainly a need to establish routines and procedures to ensure that writing workshop runs efficiently. This is particularly true in kindergarten. Establishing routines in first grade should be much easier, considering that most first graders have already had a year of writing workshop in kindergarten. A strong launching unit will help students learn the routines and procedures that help writing workshop run efficiently and will help them answer questions such as these:

- What should writing workshop sound like and look like?

- What do children do when they are finished with a piece of writing?

- How do children take responsibility for writing materials?

In kindergarten, different students write in various kinds of writing naturally (stories, list books, etc.) and we want to keep those possibilities open for first graders as well. Since many first graders will have participated in genre studies previously, we want to make sure that they don't start the year with the idea that they can write *only* in a particular genre. Therefore, it is important in some of our early minilessons during the launching unit to make sure that we are reading many different types of books during read-aloud and celebrating a range of types of student writing.

For more information on units that launch writing workshop, see the following resources:

- *About the Authors* (Ray and Cleaveland 2004)

- *Launching the Writing Workshop* (Calkins and Mermelstein 2003)

- *First Grade Writers* (Parsons 2005)

Where Writers Get Ideas

One goal for young writers is to help them realize that as writers they can choose a variety of types of topics to write about. In this unit the teacher and students read different kinds of books during read-aloud and look for information on why the authors chose to write these books. Many authors' notes give us some information as to why and how an author got the idea for the book. For example, certain editions of the book *Owl Babies* (1975) contain a note from Martin Waddell explaining how he got the idea for the book from seeing a lost child crying for his mother at the grocery store. From this kind of information, teachers can help students understand that they can write about things they see happening in their own lives.

For books in which the author's note doesn't give us information, we can talk about why we think the author might have written this book. For example, from many nonfiction books we can surmise that the author chose a topic because she knew a lot about the topic and wanted to share what she knew with others. There are also author interviews in print, on websites, and on video that tell about where writers get their ideas. The goal is that by the end of this unit the class will have opened up a wide range of writing topics and methods for generating ideas and that students will use ample strategies to ensure that they will never need to say, "I don't have anything to write about."

Using Drawing to Convey Meaning

This unit is particularly important for kindergarten students, since at the beginning of the year much of the message in their books is communicated through pictures. This unit may also be important for first grade, especially if students have not been supported in thinking strategically about their drawings.

We could easily spend the first several weeks of writing workshop teaching children specific things about drawing. The more thoughtful children are in their drawings, the better they are able to communicate meaning for their books. By helping children think about their drawings, we are also helping them think about writing. Both writing and drawing are acts of composition that require complex thinking, so the time we spend teaching drawing affects children's development as writers.

This unit is slightly different from a unit in which students study how to make illustrations work better with written text (Ray and Cleaveland 2004), since I'm not assuming that there *has* to be any written text, especially early in kindergarten. We want students to have some kind of writing on their pages as soon as possible, but the focus of this unit will be on the drawing. Children might use a range of approximations for writing such as scribble writing and random letters. We'll start working on making the writing stand on its own soon enough.

The goal for this unit is for students to think intentionally about the decisions they make as writers when drawing pictures. During this unit many of the minilessons will show students possibilities for different ways of representing people and objects in their illustrations. Possible minilessons on drawing could include the following (Horn and Giacobbe 2007; Louis 2008; Berry 2007):

- learning to draw people, animals, and objects by looking at parts and shapes

- drawing people from the side and from behind

- drawing details in clothing, hairstyles, etc.

- drawing ovals for body sections

- drawing people in action

- drawing with comparisons—some things are bigger/smaller than other things

- drawing to show distance—showing that some objects are near or far

- focusing on the most important part of the drawing with details

- drawing people with facial expressions to show emotions

- drawing people looking up and looking down

Again, the goal is to help children think intentionally about their drawings more than to teach specific drawing skills. For more detailed minilessons on teaching drawing, refer to *Talking, Drawing, Writing* (Horn and Giacobbe 2007).

Genre Overview: What Types of Books Might We Make This Year?

A unit on genres may be most appropriate for first-grade students who already have some experience with various genres. The goal of this unit is to remind (or introduce) students to the range of kinds of books they might make this year. During this unit the class would read a variety of books and talk about their characteristics (What makes realistic fiction realistic fiction, what makes nonfiction nonfiction, etc.). This unit lays the groundwork for categorizing and thinking about different types of books throughout the year. Students should be able to answer the question "What type of book are you making?" which is a very different question from "What are you writing about?" If we think back to Tom and Bryan and their train books in Chapter 2, not only did they write two different kinds of books, but they could articulate that one was a storybook while the other was a list book.

During this unit you might also show students a range of types of books that students made in previous years. Our goal is for children to learn about the types of books they will read and help them see that they can make these kinds of books as well.

Some of the types of books you might read during this unit are

- list books that tell a lot about a topic

- nonfiction books that teach people about a topic

- a range of narrative books—personal narrative, fiction, and realistic fiction

- books with a particular text structure

- poetry

While students are reading different kinds of books they will be choosing the genre in which they are writing. The simple message is that there are different kinds of books in the world, students can write in various genres, and at certain points in the year the class will study particular genres in great depth.

Reading Like a Writer

Whether teaching children to read like writers is focused around a specific unit or is embedded in units of study throughout the year, it is crucial that teachers spend time fostering this important habit of mind. Students and teachers should be having conversations about the intentional decisions authors make to write in a particular way. Students should have numerous opportunities to notice what authors do and envision how they could try the same thing in their writing.

During a unit of study focused on reading like a writer, teachers and students will read books from a variety of genres and notice and name what the author does. These noticings provide a bank of ideas for children to try out in their writing. It isn't enough to just notice what an author does. There must also be a link to the children's own writing—the idea that someone in the class could try this. The habit of noticing and thinking about how they could do it in their own writing will serve students throughout their lives as writers.

One of the keys with this unit is that the teacher selects books from a variety of genres to read with students during read-aloud. Since students are being exposed to a variety of genres and are noticing various characteristics of those genres, it is likely that students in the class will be writing in different genres. The teacher is opening up the possibilities for the types of writing students can be engaging in during this study while supporting habits of mind they will be using in specific genre studies throughout the year.

To learn more about a unit focused on reading like a writer, refer to Katie Ray and Lisa Cleaveland's book *About the Authors* (2004, 165).

In addition to the units mentioned in this chapter, I encourage you to read about the unit of study called Building a Community of Writers in Stephanie Parsons' book *First Grade Readers* (2005). It incorporates many of the issues and sentiments addressed in the units of study here, but it also focuses on children's relationships with each other as writers, something that is crucial as children create a true community of support and encouragement.

Additional Strategies for Kindergarten and First Grade

In addition to the aforementioned units of study, there are several other strategies teachers can use to maximize student energy.

- @ Oral storytelling is a natural and important early childhood skill. During the beginning of the year we also want to be supporting children's storytelling abilities by providing opportunities for students to tell stories to each other. While this can be a part of a narrative unit of study, it can also run parallel to these possible early units.

- @ Even during a genre study, students should have the opportunity to have other types of writing in their folders that they can be working on, especially if there are other types of writing for which they have more energy. For example, a child who has little energy for personal narrative writing can be writing personal narrative along with the class but have a nonfiction book in his folder that he is working on as well. The expectation will certainly be that a student does a lot of writing in the genre that is being studied. However, that doesn't mean that *all* of the writing done during that unit must be of that particular genre.

- @ There are many units of study that are not genre specific. For example, studying how authors use punctuation is a common inquiry unit. As students are studying how authors use punctuation, they are not restricted to writing in a certain genre.

- @ Throughout the rest of the year there should be open units when students are choosing to write in any genre they want. These open units often fall between regular units of study and provide children an opportunity to engage in favorite types of writing or work on a topic that they have been thinking about during other units. For example, for a child like Adrian, whom I mentioned in Chapter 2, an open unit would provide him with an opportunity to write fantasy, for which he had great interest.

When given the opportunity, whether during a unit of study or in an open unit, students will follow their own purposes as writers. During one open unit, two first graders, Jared and Colin, decided to write two separate books with the same characters. They talked about their plans for the books, and before they even started writing, they decided that their characters should meet each other in their books. Then they decided that they should combine their books into one—one story starting from the beginning and the other story starting from the end, with their characters meeting in the middle. This book required a great deal of thinking and planning, right down to making sure that the characters' clothing matched in each part of the book (see Figure 4.2 on page 68). This book was unlike any of the books either of the boys had written previously. In fact, their teacher said that it was the freedom of the open unit that led to this type of creative and unusual book. Who knows what kinds of books are inside our students, waiting to be written.

Individualized Invitations

The invitational entry points discussed in this chapter should help invite children into writing in ways that foster their energy for writing. There are many other issues related to writers who don't choose to come to the table to write or writers who come to the table and become stuck in their writing. The issues of motivation for each child are different and require a skilled teacher who knows each child well to determine how to best invite the child into writing.

Some of the children who might have a negative outlook on writing are

- children who have difficulty with fine motor tasks

- students who realize that there is a gap between their writing and conventional writing

- kids who have little letter-sound knowledge and are uncomfortable with their writing approximations

- children who have little stamina for staying with a book for very long

- students who want to write but can't think of a topic

Teachers have likely had each of these types of children in their classes. The invitational entry points discussed within this chapter will help with some of these issues, such as choosing to write or finding writing topics. Other issues come back to the big ideas that support writers, such as honoring approximations and nudging, not pushing.

If a child is not enjoying writing or thinks that writing is too hard or something she's not good at, then we need to look at our expectations for the child. We want to make sure that what we are asking the child to do is within her grasp, that it's something she can do with just a bit of support. Most frustrated

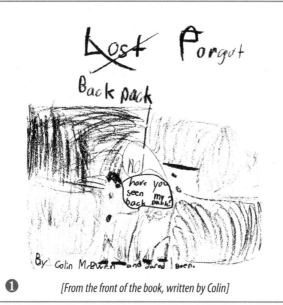

1 *[From the front of the book, written by Colin]*

"Time to go to school!!!" yelled Andrew's mom. "Do we have to?!"
Andrew groaned and yelled at the same time.
Andrew's mom just said, "Yes!"

3 Andrew ran to the bus stop like a cheetah when the bus just came.
"Whew," Andrew puffed.

When Andrew got on the bus he realized he forgot something—
his backpack!!! Everyone asked, "Where's you backpack?"

5 Andrew bumped his head into another person. "Hi. What's your
name?" asked Andrew. "My name is Luke Philip. What's your name?"
asked Luke. They have never met before.

"My name is Andrew," Andrew told Luke. "Why do you have a frown
your face?" asked Luke. Luke tried to think why he has a frown
Turn the page to hear more.

FIG. 4.2 **Excerpts from Book That Meets in the Middle**

⑦ [From the back of the book, written by Jared]

⑧

⑨ Luke ran to his class. He ran inside . . . Andrew! "Hi!"
Luke was very excited to see a familiar face.

⑩ "Where do I sit?" "There." "Cool. We get to sit by each other."
[Illustration: backpack, backpack]

FIG. 4.2 *(continued)*

writers are being asked to do things that are outside their zone of proximal development.

If teachers are thoughtful about how they invite children to enter into writing, and nurture children's images of themselves as writers, children will have the support needed to grow as writers, in both their skill and their attitude.

5

Story Entry Points

Capitalizing on Dramatic Play and Favorite Books

"You get the tent and I'll get the other stuff," said Jack.

"Let's put the tent over here," Deshawn said.

"OK. I'll start the fire," Jack said.

If you were just listening to Jack and Deshawn, you might think they were in the middle of a forest, but they were in a preschool class on a typical day in February. Their class had read several books in which the characters go camping. This led to a lot of conversation about camping and sleeping bags, so the children naturally started playing camping in the dramatic play area of the classroom. Each day their play followed a similar script. Their play also evolved over time with each retelling, becoming more sophisticated and detailed.

Similar dramatic play scenarios occur each day in the classrooms, playgrounds, and homes of young children. With a gentle nudge from a teacher, these acted-out stories can be books waiting to be written. The lure of stories, whether in dramatic play or in favorite books that have been read in class, provides powerful entry points for young writers in preschool and the primary grades.

There is a natural connection between the stories that children play and stories they have read or have heard during read-aloud. Sometimes their dramatic play is sparked by stories they know or favorite books. The combination of engaging in dramatic play, hearing stories read frequently in classrooms, and learning to write provides many opportunities for teachers to use these experiences to build on and support children's development as writers. As children play stories, hear stories, and start to write stories, they are creating an understanding of the concept of story.

In this chapter we'll consider the story entry points of dramatic play and favorite read-alouds. First, let's consider stories that children create themselves in dramatic play.

The Importance of Dramatic Play

The importance of dramatic play in early childhood is well documented (Bodrova and Leong 1996; Neuman and Roskos 2007; Owocki 1999, 2001; Bennett-Armistead, Duke, and Moses 2005). Yet children have fewer and fewer opportunities for rich, meaningful play at school at a time when they need it most. "According to Vygotsky (1966), pretend play is the leading activity of the preschool and kindergarten period because it *leads to* developmental accomplishments, such as imagination, higher-level thinking (e.g., problem solving), and self regulation. Taking away playtime may actually stunt motivation and growth such that children gain less—not more—from instruction (Panksepp, 1998)" (Neuman and Roskos 2007, 88).

Dramatic play supports children's development in numerous ways. As Armistead-Bennett, Duke, and Moses (2005, 109) point out, play allows children to

- experiment with familiar and unfamiliar roles, which helps them reinforce and consolidate their knowledge

- work through issues that are troubling them

- play with concepts and ideas to make them their own

- build literacy in ways that other classroom activities do not

Play provides opportunities for children to solve problems and develop problem-solving abilities and strategies. Vivian Paley states in *The Boy Who Would Be a Helicopter*, "Let me study your play and figure our how *play* helps you solve your problems. Play contains your questions, and I must know what questions you are asking before mine will be useful. . . . You must invent your own literature if you are to connect your ideas to the ideas of others" (1990, 18). Children's problem-solving abilities are strengthened when teachers observe children's play and notice problem-solving strategies and act on problem-solving needs.

Problem solving also fosters growth in children's language. "Children need to learn language, to hear sounds, to know the alphabet, to grasp basic print concepts, and to become interested in print. Play in early childhood supports this intellectual work. It provides a 'zone' where children can practice established skills but also reach new ones in flexible and enjoyable ways" (Neuman and Roskos 2007, 88).

Children at early ages engage in various kinds of dramatic play. They create play situations in which they act out stories themselves and take on a variety of roles. Dramatic play also encompasses stories acted out with materials such as action figures, blocks, and cars. For the purposes of this book, I use the phrase *dramatic play* to broadly encompass all of these kinds of play. Basically I consider as dramatic play any experiences where children are acting out a story in some way, whether they are the actors or whether they're using some sort of stand-in.

Children's dramatic play connects storytelling and writing quite naturally. It is not uncommon for children to tell stories based on pictures they draw. Children will draw or paint a picture and then tell an elaborate story about their picture, usually with much more detail than is represented on the page.

There is a quite natural integration of writing that takes place in many early childhood classrooms simply by placing writing materials in dramatic play areas. For example:

- The phone "rings" in the dramatic play area and a child picks up a pen and writes a phone message on a notepad next to the phone.

- When children are playing restaurant, they might order from menus written by classmates, with one of the children taking on the role of the waiter and writing down everyone's orders on a notepad.

- Children playing post office use letters, stamps, and envelopes to write letters to their friends.

- Children building a zoo out of blocks and plastic animals use paper and markers from a bin placed in the construction area to make signs for each of the animals in their zoo.

- A child uses random strings of letters to write a sign for the grocery store in the dramatic play area.

- A child picks up a clipboard with paper on it at the science center so she can record her observations of the class tadpole, using drawing and writing.

There are several ways that this type of integration of writing and play support children's writing development. Neuman and Roskos (2007, 84) offer these examples:

- Dramatic play provides opportunities for writing within the play environment.

- Dramatic play provides *more frequent* opportunities to write.

- Dramatic play provides a jumping-off place for writing compositions.

It is this third purpose that can be mined by teachers for a greater impact on children's writing when children are in a bookmaking environment. When bookmaking is a regular part of the classroom environment, then the types of compositions children create are not limited to pictures and oral retellings, play logs, or language experience charts (Neuman and Roskos 2007, 93) but can also make use of their dramatic play experience as a springboard to making books. The bookmaking experience uses skills such as retelling and drawing but nudges the child to a more complex level of thinking and composition.

This integration of natural writing into dramatic play environments should be very common in preschool classrooms, assuming that play is already a part of the preschool class. It can be easily supported by placing writing materials in the different play environments and demonstrating how they can be used as teachers engage in dramatic play with children. Integrating writing into dramatic play should happen naturally in preschool classrooms. Once incorporated, the next natural step is for children to write and make books about their dramatic play.

It is important to remember that some types of dramatic play are more beneficial than others. Some dramatic play can become overly silly, unkind, or remain at a surface level. Other dramatic play is very complex with self-defined roles and expectations. Teachers can help raise the quality of dramatic play by asking questions and making suggestions without taking over the play scenario. There is a fine line between support that nurtures play and support that becomes overly directive and takes the joy out of the play. When teachers see high-quality play, they can make a connection between the stories within children's play and the stories they write.

Supports for Dramatic Play

Dramatic play becomes more meaningful and beneficial when teachers take action to support children's dramatic play. There are several ways teachers can show students that we value dramatic play and several ways that we can support play in becoming a rich literacy experience.

- *Time.* By simply making time for dramatic play in the classroom, a teacher communicates the value of dramatic play to children. In many kindergarten and first-grade classrooms it has become more and more difficult to carve out time for dramatic play even in center time. Sadly, in some preschool classes this is also the case. By having dramatic play as a choice during a portion of the day, teachers show that they understand its importance.

- *Teacher participation.* If dramatic play is occurring in the classroom it is more likely to be productive if the teacher is involved in the play in some way. If a teacher has no involvement in the play, then he is communicating that the play isn't as important as other activities. Teachers don't have to spend huge amounts of time in dramatic play, but if they listen to children's play and make suggestions, the play will become more complex and purposeful. Even simply spending time writing down what children are saying in dramatic play will show students that we think their words are important.

@ *Sharing.* Teachers can raise the value of high-quality dramatic play in classrooms simply by talking about children's play with them, especially at group meeting or share times. At the end of the day in preschool teachers and students often talk about what students did during the day, including sharing books children made that day. Even though there may not be a tangible product after dramatic play, children can share their dramatic play stories at the end of the day the same way they would share a book. Digital pictures taken by the teacher can be a great support for students in retelling their dramatic play.

@ *Connections.* Teachers increase the value of dramatic play if they help connect children's dramatic play to other areas in the classroom. Suggesting that children paint a picture in the art center or write a book about their play helps them think more deeply about their play.

Story Entry Point: Linking Dramatic Play and Writing in Preschool

"Hurry, the alarm is going. We need to get in the truck," yelled Scott to his fellow firefighters. A group of five preschoolers scurried to get their firefighting supplies together and pile into their cardboard fire truck. Off they went to put out a fire.

This scene is similar to one that plays out in many preschool classes. For several weeks these children had been learning about fire safety and studying what firefighters do. Firefighters visited their school and the children asked them exhaustive questions about their jobs. They read books about fire trucks and fire stations as a whole class, and they also had ample opportunity to explore these books on their own. Over several weeks, they learned a lot about firefighters. As three- and four-year-olds go, they were firefighting experts.

With so much knowledge developed about firefighting, it's not surprising that they had created a fire station in their classroom in the dramatic play area, complete with a variety of props and a cardboard-box fire truck. On the day I was in their class I watched a group of children play for quite some time in this area.

They had created a fairly complex story to act out. Children had different roles and a predictable plot played out as I looked on. Kids were sitting around waiting, when suddenly Scott answered the phone. He announced that there was a fire and they all rushed to put on coats and hats. They ignored one child's suggestion to stop and get pizza on the way and hurried to put out the fire.

In watching this scene, it was obvious that they had lived this story before and knew how the story should progress. The fact that this group of children knew this story so well made it a prime candidate to turn into a book. So, as they were returning home from a hard day of firefighting, I started to talk with them about what they had just done. I asked them questions about how they had put out the fire and how they had learned so much about firefighters. They eagerly shared their knowledge. Finally, I sprung the question:

"Do you think you could make a book about what you just did?"

"Yes," four children enthusiastically responded.

"No," said Dylan, who was more interested in continuing to play.

That type of reaction is common for several reasons. First, when children know a story well and have already lived it, sharing their story on paper is a much easier and more interesting endeavor. It's also not uncommon for children to choose not to write a book. Perhaps it wasn't what Dylan wasn't interested in doing right then. Perhaps he had made a book the day before. Whatever the reason, if I'd pushed too hard I would have reduced his potential energy for making a book.

As it turned out, I didn't need to push at all. As soon as Dylan saw that his friends were going to make books, he decided to join them, which isn't surprising, since for young children writing is a very social process. If several children are at the writing center, they are often joined by several others, in the same way that if two children are playing fire station, they often attract the interest and participation of a few other children.

This group of children didn't bother to take off their firefighting hats and coats—they immediately got busy making books. It was easy to see that making books was a normal part of what they did in their class, so they didn't need much support to get going. They worked on their books for ten minutes or so until it was time to clean up. Their books represented the typical range of books we'd see written by young children, and they looked like they were written by three- and four-year-old children. Books like Dylan's in Figure 5.1 provide us with clear ideas about how and where to nudge students' composition or word-making development. For example, I could choose to help Dylan add details to his illustrations, or I could ask him to add words in his own approximated way, or I could help him incorporate some story language into his reading of his book.

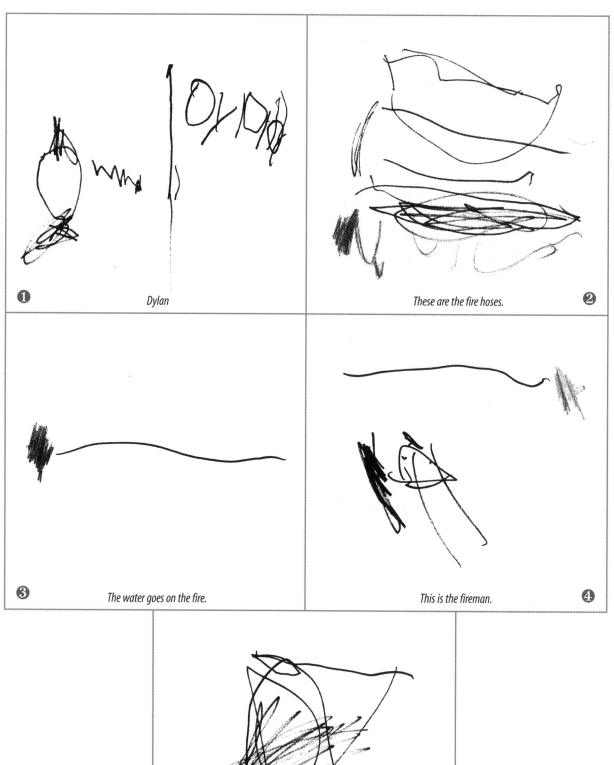

1 — Dylan

2 — These are the fire hoses.

3 — The water goes on the fire.

4 — This is the fireman.

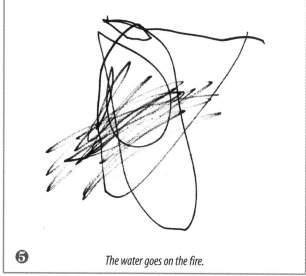

5 — The water goes on the fire.

FIG. 5.1 **Dylan's Book About Firefighting**

There are several things that are useful to understand about this dramatic play scenario in thinking about transferring stories from dramatic play into bookmaking:

- Children's energy for writing was high. It didn't take a lot of nudging to get them started and to sustain their efforts.

- They were in an environment where the suggestion to go make a book occurred naturally and frequently.

- More-reluctant writers were drawn into the writing experience in natural, unforced ways.

- The writing experience was relatively easy for them since they were writing about something they knew well, something they had already lived. Basically, their books were written before they came to the writing center.

- The goal wasn't for the children to accurately re-create the exact sequence of events in their play. There wasn't even an expectation that their books should be written as stories. Their books could have been written just as easily as list books telling all about firefighting equipment (e.g., This is a fire truck. This is the hose.) or the story of putting out a fire (e.g., We got in the fire truck. We drove to the fire.). As expected, their books had a very approximated quality to them.

Certainly more energy and thinking were invested by these children in their stories than if they had colored in a photocopied picture of a fire truck book or simply created a class book about fire safety, for example. In preschool classrooms there should be ample opportunity for rich, purposeful dramatic play that is supported by teachers and can lead to rich writing experiences.

Dramatic Play in the Primary Grades

In today's world, academics are pushed at increasingly early ages, and dramatic play in kindergarten or first grade can unfortunately be pushed aside. "Many preschools and kindergartens have reduced or even eliminated playtime from their schedules in favor of more structured language and literacy lessons (Zigler & Bishop-Josef, 2004)" (Neuman and Roskos 2007, 87). In my experience, primary-grade teachers who don't nurture active dramatic play that supports writing work in their classrooms tend to fall into one several categories:

- Teachers who don't have any dramatic play opportunities in classrooms either because they have been squeezed out by the push for academic standards or because the teachers don't see value in them.

- Teachers who have dramatic play areas because they feel they are developmentally appropriate but aren't quite sure how to support them. These areas are then used infrequently by children or not to their potential.

- Teachers who have active, well-used dramatic play areas, but with little link to writing.

Teachers hoping to expand dramatic play in their classroom might create areas that support dramatic play beyond the traditional house setup. Also, dramatic play may occur in early childhood classrooms where teachers and children have created a new area as part of a project, such as creating a bakery in the classroom as part of a study of bakeries.

Whether or not dramatic play is sanctioned and supported by kindergarten and first-grade teachers, it is likely that many kindergarten and first-grade children are engaging in dramatic play at school. Many children spend their recess time engaged in elaborate pretend play, acting out stories they create or stories they know from movies, television, and books.

I know a kindergarten teacher who manages to skillfully balance the worlds of intellectual and academic development. She provides her students with excellent literacy instruction, unique art experiences, and opportunities that push them to think in creative ways. At one point in the year, several of the students in this class had been playing with a toy house and people near the block and construction area of her classroom. The teacher started observing more closely what was happening in this area. She started transcribing the stories children were playing. She would occasionally reread to children what they had been saying. So, it was quite natural for this teacher to make the suggestion that children make a book about the story they had already written when playing.

Figure 5.2 shows a portion of a transcript of several children's play with the toy house. Matthew's book is one that was linked to this play. At this point in his writing development, Matthew was the kind of writer who would use just one page and keep adding and adding and adding to that page. Despite encouragement, he was not yet stretching his stories across pages, and it was equally difficult for him to bring his stories to a close.

During writing workshop his teacher suggested that children could write about their play with the house. She read one of their transcribed play scripts and showed them how they could plan their story across blank pages. During independent writing that day Matthew wrote the book you see in Figure 5.3 on page 80. This book was dramatically different from his previous books. He easily wrote across pages and ended it on his own, which was an easier process since this was a story he knew well. Furthermore, his newfound ability transferred to his subsequent books.

Dramatic Play Log—Alex, Courtney, Matthew

Alex: You're the mom and I'm the papaw. I'm fixing the roof. Can you give me the ladder, guys?

Courtney: *[Using the vacuum, mop, cleaning as Alex narrates]*

Alex: I'm up here fixing it. I can't get down.

Matthew: Where are the steps?

Alex: I need help. I'm going to fall!

Matthew: I'll help you!

Alex: I'm falling. *[Man slides off the roof.]* Ohhhh!

Matthew: I'm on the roof. I'm stuck. I can't get off!

Alex: Don't fall.

Matthew: I'm falling, too. I'm hurt!

Alex: We have to get fixed at the hospital!

Matthew: Let's go to the hospital.

FIG. 5.2 *Play Transcript*

The books sparked by play in this class were not limited to the block area. Several of the children were engaged in elaborate play scenarios on the playground. Evan and some friends played *Star Wars* on the playground. When asked, Evan could explain their play in great detail and how they used certain pieces of playground equipment for certain things in their play, such as the fireman's pole for the part when someone falls in the deep hole.

During a minilesson in writing workshop in which the goal was to talk about how children could turn dramatic play into books, Evan talked about playing *Star Wars* on the playground with his friends. With a little support, he planned out what would go on each page of his book. Again, this was fairly easy for him since he had already written this story, so to speak, on the playground. This type of experience also tapped into a natural entry point into writing for Evan. He was a dramatic play type of kid, the type of kid who often acted out all sorts of things. When I talked with his mother about his writing, she said that Evan had spent much of the past few days acting out the latest Bengals-Steelers football game in their

① Mom and Dad are on the roof. The ladder falls.

② They fall down. "I'm falling."

③ They went to the hospital in the hospital car.

④ He's in bed with a broken leg and stitches.

FIG. 5.3 *Matthew's Book About Playing House*

living room, complete with slow-motion replays. For children like Evan, dramatic play is an effective springboard into writing. (See Figure 5.4 on page 81.)

While Evan was playing *Star Wars*, McKenzie and her friends were playing Tinkerbell. If you were just watching McKenzie and her friends on the playground, you might think that they were just running around. But if you asked McKenzie about their play, she would tell you exactly why they were running to various places and why some people ran before others. What looked like random running was actually much more complex. It makes you wonder how many stories are being written on playgrounds and in backyards each day that adults don't know about.

❶ *Darth Vader and Luke Skywalker*

❷ *"I will still beat you."*
[One sound per word: t in beat and u for you.]

❸ *"Ahhhh," he screamed really loud*

❹ *This is the ship.*

❺ *Three, two, one, blastoff. And they blast off to space.*

FIG. 5.4 **Evan's Star Wars Book**

Both of these scenarios were played over several days. They had characters and a basic plot structure. All of the elements were there for the play to grow into books: the kids had written stories in dramatic play, they had a teacher who was observing carefully what was occurring on the playground, and the classroom environment had a strong writing workshop where students made books on a regular basis. It only took a small suggestion from the teacher that they could write a book about what they were playing for each of them to enthusiastically respond.

In watching children's dramatic play closely, this same teacher noticed several connections that point to the benefits of linking dramatic play and writing in primary-grade classrooms.

- The children who were writing books sparked from their playground stories were playing differently both in the classroom and on the playground. They became more precise and purposeful in their play, with more specific details, characters, and plots. There was a very reciprocal, interdependent relationship between their play and their writing. Their play sparked their writing, which in turn supported the quality of their play, which then positively affected their writing, and so on.

- When other children heard children's play stories when they shared their writing, they wanted to become involved in them, too, leading to more writing possibilities for more children.

- Children's story language became more sophisticated, both in their play and in their writing.

- For children who had a difficult time finding writing topics, writing about their dramatic play gave them a story they already knew.

- Different groups of children's dramatic play stories started to merge. As children heard each other's stories (something that hadn't happened before), they started to incorporate language and actions from each other's stories. Their stories became a more collaborative, social composition.

- On their own, children started giving their dramatic play stories titles, just like they might with a written book, which shows that they were thinking more about their stories' content. The title of one of their play stories was "Haunted House," which Cameron revised to "Haunted House Creepy Revenge" because he thought the first title wasn't "monsterly" enough.

- Children also developed a deeper sense of character development in their dramatic play. Children's play characters started staying the same from day to day with more detailed, consistent characteristics developing as time passed.

It should be noted that dramatic play might be a writing springboard for only some of the children in your classroom. Like each of the entry points described in this book, dramatic play will interest some children more than others. In the classroom described here, a minority of the students were engaged in and writing about dramatic play. If we were to require all children to write books stemming from their dramatic play, we would be limiting them as much as if we were telling them they could write only nonfiction or only about true things that happened to them. However, for this group of students, some of whom had difficulty generating writing topics and writing independently, dramatic play helped them make significant strides early in their kindergarten year.

Dramatic play is not limited to preschool and kindergarten. Older children in third and fourth grade also engage in recess-time dramatic play. They pretend to be spies and superheroes and soldiers. While their play is different than that of younger children, and it is clearly taking place outside the realm of the sanctioned school day, it shows that some children are natural story makers. If they can do it one context, teachers can help them translate that experience into books.

Story Entry Point: Connecting Favorite Read-Alouds and Writing

Understanding the idea of story is a natural entry point for children. Just as children naturally play, many children have favorite books that they love to hear over and over again or books they love to read themselves. Very familiar picture books provide children with a story that they already know and have internalized, much like the stories developed by dramatic play. Teachers deepen this understanding of story when they read favorite books repeatedly and help children explore them in more depth. Given children's connection with favorite books, it simply isn't surprising that stories and characters children love and know well will start to appear in the books children make.

The difference between stories inspired by children's dramatic play and stories inspired by favorite books is that children are generally creating their own dramatic play stories while students' books inspired by favorite read-alouds interpret a story someone else has created. Books help connect children's world of play with the world of writing, so we'll look at how to support that in both preschool and the primary grades.

Deep understanding of stories in well-loved books helps children see how stories play out across pages, something they don't see in their own dramatic play. Teachers can help bridge children's dramatic play and their writing by helping children see how stories work in the written form of a book. Making these connections can be done very subtly. For example: "When we were reading *Whopper Cake* [Wilson 2006] it reminded me of when Demarco and Lily were playing in the bakery. They were getting all of the things they needed and talking about what they would make today, like how the man got all of the ingredients for the cake in *Whopper Cake*."

There are some types of books that particularly lend themselves to repeated reading and deep engagement. Children will decide which books they love and want to have read over and over again, but teachers can help get the ball rolling through the types of stories they read. The following types of books help children connect published books and their writing:

- Books with *memorable, engaging characters* that children can relate to. Most children can relate to the feeling of losing a beloved toy like Trixie in *Knuffle Bunny* (Willems 2004).

- Books that *can easily be acted out*. Many classic fairy tales, like *Three Billy Goats Gruff* (e.g., Galdone 1981), are easy for children to reenact. Many fairy tales have repeated dialogue or patterned language, like *The Three Little Pigs* (e.g., Marshall 2000), which make them easy for children to remember.

- Books with *interesting actions*. *Going on a Bear Hunt* (Rosen 1989) is a favorite book for preschool children to act out while they're reading it or on their own afterward.

- Series of books with *the same characters*. Deep engagement isn't limited to books that can be acted out. The Pigeon books by Mo Willems are interactive but become valuable to understanding story when students begin to know a character, the pigeon, well and start to predict how he will act in each story.

- Books that have *a broad appeal* for the children in your class. As teachers we must constantly keep in mind that students have experiences that may be different from our own when selecting books that will be of interest to all children in the class.

Children will find books they love if teachers take the time to reread and delve deeply into great books.

Favorite Read-Alouds in Preschool

In one preschool class the students loved the book *Owl Babies*, by Martin Waddell (1975), the story of three baby owls nervously waiting for their mother to return to the nest. They loved reading the book over and over and joining in with the baby owl Bill as he cried for his mom. They acted the story out during group time, with students taking turns being the mother and each of the owl babies. As they acted it out the teacher supported them in using some of the dialogue from the book. Children naturally started acting it out on their own during choice time. It became a story children knew inside and out, much like the student-created dramatic play stories we've already examined.

Given how much they loved the book, it's not surprising that versions of *Owl Babies* started to appear in the writing center. These were not necessarily created at the suggestion of the teacher; she didn't say, "You could go make your own *Owl Babies* books." Perhaps because children could so clearly see the connection between a book they read and the books they made, it was natural that they started making their own versions of *Owl Babies*, such as Cecelie's book in Figure 5.5 on page 86.

One of the key conditions that is necessary for literature to become a spark for writing is an understanding of the power of multiple readings of books. Educators such as Dorothy Strickland and Elizabeth Sulzby have promoted the idea that teachers and children should read some books more than once. Books should be read multiple times in order for children to internalize them. Reading a book once and then moving on to another the next day simply doesn't provide children with the opportunity to think more deeply about a book.

This doesn't mean that every book is read more than once. Children should be hearing multiple books a day and many of the books they hear will be read once and then be available in the class library. But some carefully selected books will have the distinction of being read multiple times.

Sometimes the books preschoolers make are retellings, but sometimes children simply borrow characters or ideas and create their own books. If children read all of Mo Willems' Pigeon books or Melanié Watt's Scaredy Squirrel books, they start to know characters and their traits well. The more thoroughly a child knows a character, the more likely it will be that that character will show up in her own writing.

That's what happened in Luke's preschool class. The teacher and students had read *Little Blue and Little Yellow*, by Leo Lionni (1994), several times and loved the book. They knew the story well and its simple pictures made it especially accessible to young children. It wasn't surprising that Luke decided to make

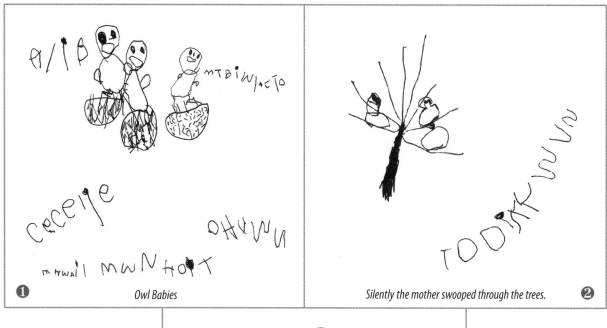

① *Owl Babies*

② *Silently the mother swooped through the trees.*

③ *The mother was back home with her babies.*

FIG. 5.5 *Cecelie's "Owl Babies" Book*

his own book about Little Blue and Little Yellow sparked by his interest in Leo Lionni's book. (See Figure 5.6.)

Another preschool class had been looking at pop-up books, especially the ones by author David E. Carter. I know this because when I sat down next to Nate one day, he explained that he was trying to make a book where you find things in the picture. I asked him if he had gotten this idea from Blake, another boy in his class who was trying to make pop-up books and had discovered how to make lift-the-flap books by taping an index card on each page of his book. Nate said, "Yes, but I also learned from David E. Carter. He's an author."

1. *This is Little Blue, Yellow, and Green running down the street.*

2. *They were climbing up the mountain.*

3. *Little Green was trapped.*
   They're looking everywhere for Little Green.

4.

FIG. 5.6 **Luke's Book About Little Blue**

As we talked he explained that he wanted his reader to find a red dot on each page and would hide it under a flap. I asked him how he would let his reader know what color to find, especially if he wasn't nearby to tell them. Nate replied that he would write "one red dot" on the cover so readers would know what to find. It's difficult to get the full effect of Nate's book here without being able to see that the dots are different colors or being able to lift the flaps, but Figure 5.7 on page 88 shows some of the pages from the book with the flaps both down and up.

Both Luke and Nate were students in classrooms with teachers who talked about authors on a regular basis. Students in these classrooms knew the types of

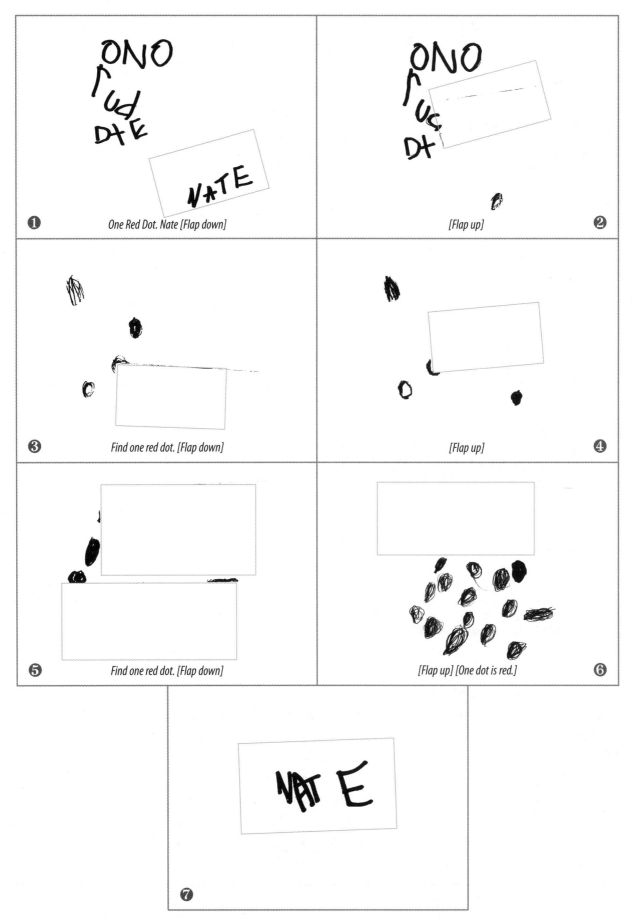

FIG. 5.7 *Excerpts from Nate's "One Red Dot" Book*

books authors make. An understanding of specific authors helped each boy develop his own image of himself as an author, the type of person who could make a book like Leo Lionni or David E. Carter.

Favorite Books in the Primary Grades

Like books based on dramatic play, books stemming from favorite read-alouds are not limited to preschool. In fact, depending on the types of units of study in kindergarten and first-grade classrooms, they may even be more common in those grades than in preschool.

Stewart was a first grader who didn't enjoy writing. He would write each day in writing workshop, but not with much energy, enthusiasm, or stamina. Writing was not easy for him at the beginning of the year and he struggled to come up with writing topics. Early in the year his class had been writing personal narratives and Stewart felt that this was the only type of writing he could do. When a literacy specialist in the school mentioned some ideas Stewart might write about, he said he was only supposed to write about true things that had happened to him, which for Stewart was not very energizing.

A couple of months into the year, Stewart's teacher launched a study of one of the children's favorite authors, Mo Willems. They immersed themselves in Mo's books and noticed the writing moves Mo made in his books. They listed their noticings on a chart and tried many of those moves in their own writing. One thing their teacher didn't say was "You could write your own Knuffle Bunny book." But Stewart, like the other children in the class, had developed an ability to read like a writer, so Stewart figured he could try writing Knuffle Bunny–type stories of his own.

Stewart changed Bunny to Bob, and his series of Knuffle Bob books was born. The Knuffle Bob books were basically retellings of Mo Willems' books *Knuffle Bunny* (2004) and *Knuffle Bunny Too* (2007). But with each new book Stewart departed a bit more from the books he had read and added more of his own ideas. You can see the covers of his four Knuffle Bob books in Figure 5.8 on page 90. What can't be seen in these covers is the change in Stewart's attitude and energy for writing. By writing about something he enjoyed and escaping the bounds of personal narrative, Stewart began to see himself as the type of person who could write stories to entertain his classmates. He began to have an image of himself as an author, like Mo Willems, who liked to write stories that would entertain his friends. He quickly outgrew his Knuffle Bob books and throughout the year wrote a variety of original, increasingly sophisticated books.

I want to be clear that I'm certainly not encouraging every child in a class to retell stories he has read. We want children to generate their own topics and

FIG. 5.8 *Stewart's Knuffle Bob Covers*

ideas. Like many teachers, I become a bit uneasy when a child is only writing other people's stories or retelling a favorite movie for the fifteenth time. I want to nudge kids into their own writing identities rather than let them only assume the identities of other authors. However, we first want to support topics that give a child the most motivation and energy for writing. In this case, I wonder if without these book topics, the students' growth as writers would have been more difficult. And after all, many experienced authors are inspired by fellow authors. If we are talking frequently about published authors and studying closely the deci-

ENGAGING YOUNG WRITERS

sions they make, it won't be surprising if some of children's writing stems from books they have read.

The Importance of Talk, Again

One final thought on the importance of dramatic play and favorite read-alouds: they support children's oral language development. Children need lots and lots of opportunities to talk, and to talk in productive ways. As children hear rich language in books read aloud, they are hearing more sophisticated language than they might typically use. When they hear this type of language it is likely that they will start to use it in their play and eventually in their writing. When children hear books read aloud and act out their own stories, they are growing an understanding of story language, characters, and concepts of story.

This connection between oral language, dramatic play, and books is particularly important in today's society, where it seems that children spend less and less time engaged in play and have fewer opportunities to talk. While as teachers we can't control what happens outside of school, we do control what happens within our classroom environments. Utilizing the power of story through dramatic play and read-alouds, teachers can create rich language environments for children that encourage them to think, talk, play, and write in ways that show deep engagement and understanding.

6

Experience Entry Points

You Could Make a Book About That

In late December I was in our school cafeteria while Emma's first-grade class was lining up to go back to its classroom from lunch. I was talking with the children in Emma's class about a variety of things as I slowly walked along their line. When I got to Emma I remembered that over the weekend she had danced in *The Nutcracker* at the studio where she took dance lessons. I asked Emma how the performance went and Emma started telling me about the performance and all that she and her friend Abby had done.

I commented that Emma sure knew a lot about ballet. Then I said, "Emma, have you written about this yet?" Emma said she hadn't but was thinking that she might. I suggested that if she did, she could write about it in a way that would tell people about what she did as well as teach people some things about ballet. We talked about some ideas for how she could do this and then it was time for her class to leave. The whole conversation took only a minute or so. I wasn't expecting that Emma would actually decide to write this book and didn't think much more about it.

A couple of days later Emma showed up at my office with her book about dancing in *The Nutcracker* (see Figure 6.1). One of the things that is interesting about her book is that she writes much more about getting ready for the performance than the actual dance itself. While I might have encouraged her to write more about the dance or how she felt right before going on stage, I shouldn't have been surprised that the time leading up to the dance was the focus, since for a six-year-old girl the excitement is all in getting ready for the dance and what happens after dancing. But what was more interesting to me was how easily Emma wrote about this experience and how she tried to teach her reader some facts about ballet. When I had made this suggestion I hadn't realized that her class had been reading books like *Gentle Giant Octopus*, by Karen Wallace (2002), and had noticed how some authors embed facts about their

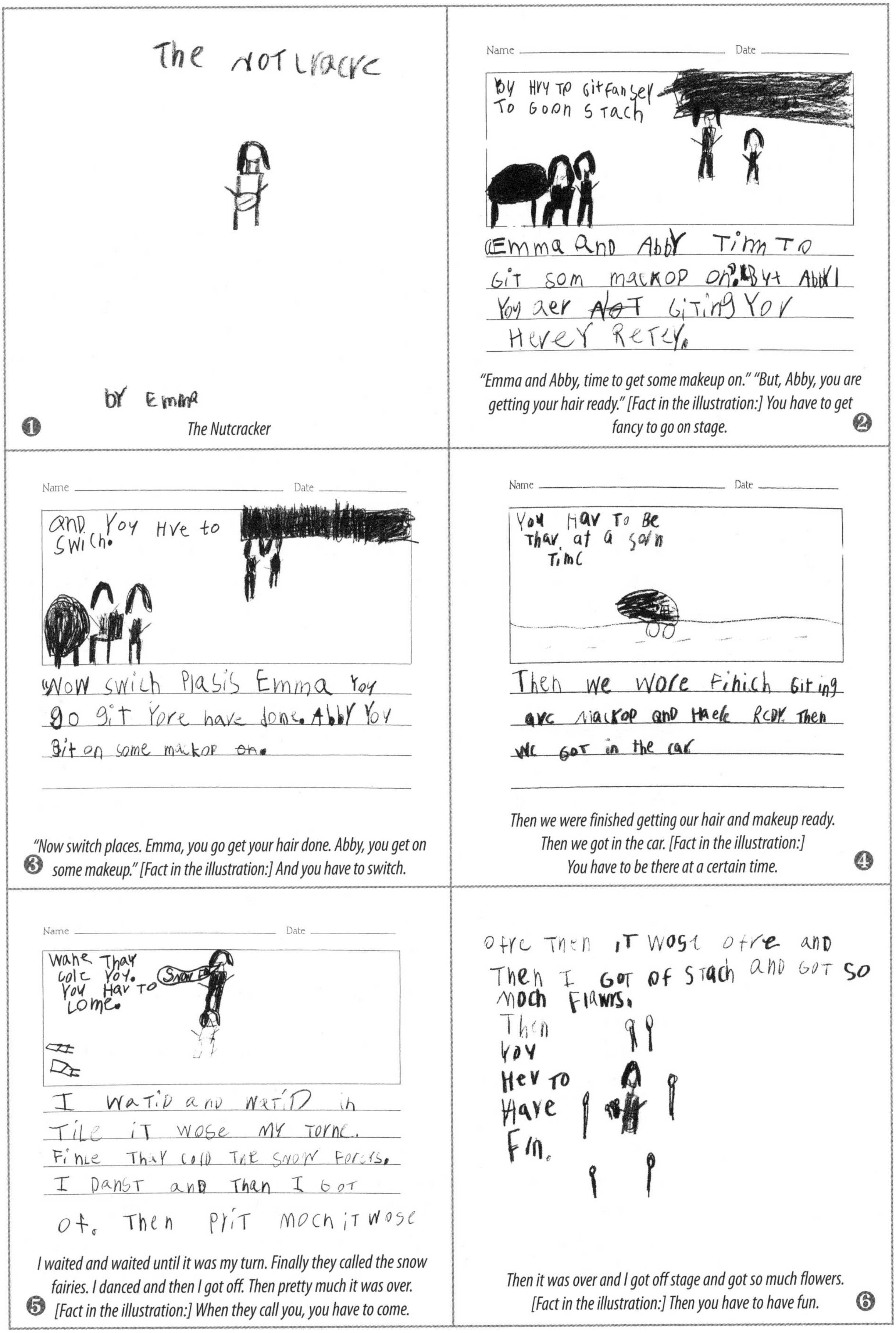

Panel 1:

The NOTLRACYC

by Emma

The Nutcracker

Panel 2:

Name _____ Date _____

BY HRY TO GiTFANSEY
TO GOON STACH

EMMA anD AbbY TiM TO
GiT SOM MAEKOP ON. BYt AbiXi
YOY aeR AloT GiTiNG YOV
HEVEY RETEY.

"Emma and Abby, time to get some makeup on." "But, Abby, you are getting your hair ready." [Fact in the illustration:] You have to get fancy to go on stage.

Panel 3:

Name _____ Date _____

AND YOY HVe to
SWiCh.

WOW SWiCh PlaSiS EMMa YoY
go giT Yore have done. AbbY YoV
BiT on some maKoP On.

"Now switch places. Emma, you go get your hair done. Abby, you get on some makeup." [Fact in the illustration:] And you have to switch.

Panel 4:

Name _____ Date _____

YoU HaV To Be
Thar. at a Sa'n
TimC

Then we wore Fihich GiTing
aVe MacKoP anD HaeR RCDY. Then
WC GoT in the caR

Then we were finished getting our hair and makeup ready. Then we got in the car. [Fact in the illustration:] You have to be there at a certain time.

Panel 5:

Name _____ Date _____

Wahe Thay
coLc YoY.
YoU HaV To
LoME.
SNOW

I WATiD anD WaTiD in
TiLe iT WoSe MY ToRne.
FiNLe ThaY coLD ThE SNOW FeReis.
I DanST anD Than I GoT
oF. Then PriT MoCh iT WoSe

I waited and waited until it was my turn. Finally they called the snow fairies. I danced and then I got off. Then pretty much it was over. [Fact in the illustration:] When they call you, you have to come.

Panel 6:

OFrC THen iT WoST oFre anD
THen I GoT oF STACH anD GoT So
MoCh FlaWiS.
Then
YoY
HeV To
HaVe
FiN.

Then it was over and I got off stage and got so much flowers. [Fact in the illustration:] Then you have to have fun.

FIG. 6.1 *Emma's Book About The Nutcracker*

topic in their illustrations. Emma was simply trying this out in her book after a very casual suggestion.

Writing about experiences is an engaging entry point for some young writers since they are writing about something they already know. One of the early working titles for this book was *You Could Make a Book About That*. A bit wordy, but it captures the sentiment that book topics are right in front of us and the children we work with each day if we just notice them. The short hallway conversation with Emma led to a book topic that she easily wrote about with a great deal of motivation and energy. For Emma, writing about this experience provided an entry point into the writing process, an entry point that she cared about, that was meaningful, and that was engaging.

One of the great things about working with young children is that they eagerly come up to adults and tell us the most interesting things. On many days I'm in the hallway or outside as students are coming into school. More often than not a child will come up to me and without any pragmatic lead-in declare something like, "You know what, Mr. Glover? Last night my dog threw up in my bedroom." The child tells me his important thought and then just as quickly heads off to his classroom. Teachers of young children know this type of scenario well, since it plays out in early childhood classrooms every day. It's as if the child just *has* to tell someone, anyone, this thought and now that it's been told, he can move on to the next part of his day.

Recognizing Topics

A child's day is full of many potential entry points into writing. After thinking about writing so much over the past several years, whenever I hear one of these stories, almost without thinking, I will say something like, "Wow, you know that would be a great book. You could make a book about that." I often describe it as having a sickness that leads to my "you could make a book about that" response. I just can't help myself. There's an expression that goes something like "When you're a hammer, everything looks like a nail." That's the way I've become with children and book topics.

Now, don't worry that I suggest she write a book every time one of my four-year-old daughters tells me about something amazing she has found in the back-yard or something that happened at preschool that day. I am able to leave my sickness at school, at least for the most part.

There are book topics everywhere if we start looking for them. As teachers and parents, we can help children find potential book topics in the big and little things they do each day. When teachers see this potential, it's not surprising that children start thinking about books and book topics outside of their school day, just like more experienced writers think about their writing topics outside of their writing time. Writers, experienced or inexperienced, can think about books at any time.

So while I'm not constantly suggesting book topics to my daughters Molly and Natalie, there are times at home when I suggest to my daughters that they might write a book about something that has happened. We have lots of conversations about potential books, some of which turn into actual books and many of which don't. What's been interesting about this is that over time, Molly and Natalie just kind of naturally think about things in terms of books. When we go on a trip they will often say something like, "This will be a good part to put in my book." For example, when we made our annual trip to a Wake Forest basketball game, Molly and Natalie were anticipating the player introductions when the lights would go out and the Demon Deacon mascot would come out on his motorcycle (much more exciting than the actual game if you're four years old). Right after this happened, Natalie leaned over and said, "I'm going to put this part in my book. I'm going to have to use lots of black marker to show that it's dark." On that day I hadn't suggested making a book, but she simply had anticipated that at some point she'd be making a book about her trip and she might want to include this part. Of course by the time we got back home she may have decided to include different parts about the game, if she even decided to make a book at all. What's important isn't whether she made a book or not. What's significant is that at four she was thinking like someone who was going to make a book about what she was doing.

Supporting Thinking About Experiences

When children are thinking about books and book topics like this, we can support their thinking in natural ways. One of the most important and natural supports we can provide as teachers and parents is to simply talk with children about books they could make during times when they aren't writing. For example, one of the classes at our school had taken a field trip to a pumpkin farm. On the bus ride home the teacher was talking with some students about what they did on the farm. This could have been a typical conversation about what they did at the farm, what their favorite part was, and so on. But this teacher made one subtle teaching move that changed the nature of this conversation. She said, "If you were going to make a book about going to the pumpkin farm, what would go on the first page?" The following conversation ensued.

"The first page would be about going on the hayride," Devon said.

"How are you going to draw that?" asked the teacher.

"Well, I think I'm going to draw the whole wagon with all of us sitting in it."

After some conversation about whom Devon would need to include in her illustration, the teacher asked, "What is going to go on the next page?"

Devon said, "That will be the part where we saw all of the pumpkins lined up."

The teacher asked, "Did that happen before or after we went on the hayride?"

Devon thought for a moment and said, "We saw all of those pumpkins when we first got there."

Gently the teacher nudged, "Oh, do you think that should go on the first page or the second page?"

"Well, that should probably go on the first page."

You can imagine how the conversation went as the teacher and the child talked about the sequence of her book. Whether she ultimately decided to write this book or not, this prewriting conversation was valuable. Think about the writing goals that were addressed in this casual exchange.

- *Composing*—thinking about what you are going to include in a book

- *Sequencing*—deciding on the order of events in a narrative (which is not always easy for young children)

- *Adding details*—more detailed drawing can lead to more detailed writing

- *Prewriting*—thinking ahead about what will be in your book

- *Revision*—you can change the order of things in your book

Addressing these types of goals in natural conversations with children provides support for their thinking about writing outside of a formal writing context. The more frequently students think about bookmaking, the easier it will be when they actually write.

Topics Big and Small

Lilian Katz, who is an expert on the subject of selecting topics for whole-class projects, talks about how teachers should avoid being seduced by the exotic: "Such projects that involve young children in investigating real phenomena offer them an opportunity to be the natural scientists or anthropologists that they seem to be born to be. On the other hand, if the topic of a project is exotic and outside of the children's direct experience, they are dependent on the teacher for most of the questions, ideas, information, thinking and planning" (Edwards, Gandini, and Forman 1998, 33). She tells of classes that study topics like the rainforest, for which children have little if any firsthand knowledge, when they could be studying the ravine near their school. I see this when young children study things like penguins. Not many children in Ohio come into contact with penguins in their everyday lives. But they do come into contact with squirrels and creeks—topics that they could observe, study, and research on a firsthand basis.

Similar cautions apply to book topic selection. Events don't need to be huge and grand in order to be considered as book topics. Sometimes teachers and students think of big events for book topics and miss the numerous everyday events that could be written about just as easily.

It's natural to think of big events—birthdays, trips, soccer games—for book topics. By nature they're easy to write about because children have a lot of interest in them and they're memorable. However, children can write about small, everyday events as well. In fact, one of the messages we want to convey to young children is that they can write about any event, big or small.

One of the problems with suggesting small topics is that children don't usually come into school talking about these everyday events. They don't usually say, "Guess what, Mr. Glover, I ate breakfast this morning." They tend to remember the more unusual or special occurrences in their lives. And, eating breakfast isn't always the most interesting thing to write about. Writers look for topics that might interest their readers.

But what about the children in our schools who don't have big events to write about? As Stephanie Jones, author of *Girls, Social Class and Literacy: What Teachers Can Do to Make a Difference* (2006), reminded me after she read *Already Ready* (Ray and Glover 2008), all children don't go to the zoo or have birthday parties. We don't want to communicate to children, or teachers, that you can write only about big events. Sometimes children with fewer experiences feel they need to make up stories to match the experiences of their classmates. We need to help students see the value and worth of any topic of interest.

Building on Experiences at School

One of the best ways to help all children find topics, regardless of experiences outside of school, is to encourage them to write about things that happen when they are at school. We control what happens in our classrooms (at least as much as anyone has control over what happens with a group of three- to seven-year-olds), so our classrooms should be places where interesting things happen. If they aren't, we should reconsider the types of classrooms we're creating.

The other advantage of writing about events that happen when teachers are present, as opposed to writing about things that happen at home, is that teachers can support children in remembering the sequence of the events as they write.

We also need to remember that what might be unremarkable to adults might be highly interesting to a child. The day that a class of preschoolers made popcorn for their daily snack provided one of those events. What made this popcorn experience different was that they made popcorn in an "old-fashioned" popcorn popper, the kind you put oil in that has a yellow plastic top that doubles as a bowl. The children had never seen popcorn that didn't come from a microwave, so this experience served the dual purpose of being a new experience and making me feel very old.

I came into the class as the students and teacher were eating their popcorn. I sat down and asked them where they had gotten such delicious popcorn. Without any prompting came the replies:

"We made it in a real popcorn maker, the old kind."

"We put oil and popcorn in and it got real hot."

"The popcorn spinned round and round."

"When it was finished we ate it."

After their initial onslaught of comments I asked some follow-up questions to clarify the procedure for making old-fashioned popcorn. From time to time the teacher joined in the conversation to help fill in vocabulary (e.g., *kernels*) and gaps in the sequence for popping popcorn. We talked for a bit while we ate, and then at the end I simply stated, "I wonder if any of you might make a book about making popcorn." Several said they might, including Bryn. (See Figure 6.2).

As I watched Bryn I wasn't surprised that she wrote this book easily and without much assistance because

- she made the decision to write;

- she chose the topic;

- making popcorn was a topic of interest;

- it was a topic she could talk easily about; and

- before starting to write, she rehearsed the story as she talked about making popcorn.

Because Bryn was in a classroom environment where making different kinds of books was a common occurrence, it was very natural for her and her friends to write books about their popcorn experience.

It is not unusual for preschool and kindergarten students to write about something that has not yet happened but write about it as if it has occurred. The whole concept of time is challenging for very young writers. Trying to figure out if something happened yesterday, last week, last month, or last year can be an interesting

1 We made popcorn.

2 First you put in the oil.

3 Then you put in the popcorn.

4 We waited for it to pop.

5 Pop, pop, pop, pop, pop, pop, pop, pop, pop, pop.

6 We ate it. It was good.

FIG. 6.2 **Bryn's Book About Popcorn**

conversation with a four-year-old. One of the advantages of writing about experiences that happen at school is that we know the context and details and can help students start to understand these concepts. However, we don't limit students to these types of topics, of course, because we want students to choose topics for which they have the most energy.

A Classroom of Possibilities

Topics for books appear in our classrooms and homes each day; we just need to remember to look for them. The following are some common classroom experiences that children might write about:

- yesterday's fire drill

- what they did during center time with a friend

- carving a pumpkin in the class

- playing on the playground

- the fireman's visit to the classroom

- the blue squishy bag they made in the science center

- going to the school library

- playing with the class pet hamster

If classroom experiences aren't sparking writing, then we need to be looking more at the types of experiences children are having rather than trying to find writing topics. If our classrooms are interesting places, and they should be, writing topics will follow.

Observing Purposefully

Writing about an experience can be particularly powerful for a child who isn't choosing to write or who doesn't know what to write about. I often go into preschool classes and ask the teacher if there is a child who hasn't been choosing to write. One of the strategies I typically employ is to simply watch the child for a while during choice time to see what she is choosing to do. While some children might not be choosing to write, they are choosing to do something in the classroom during choice time, and whatever that is has potential to become a writing topic. This was the strategy I decided to use when I went into Jacob's preschool classroom.

I knew that Jacob wasn't regularly choosing to write and didn't quite have an image of himself as someone who could make a book. It wasn't that he didn't want to write, but he would say he didn't have anything to write about or that he couldn't write. So on this day I simply watched Jacob for a while during choice time. Jacob checked out what was going on in several centers before deciding on the block area, where another student, Heather, was already playing. I watched the two of them build a tall tower that eventually crashed. They picked up the pieces and started to reconstruct their tower. I watched as they built for ten minutes or so. In addition to learning some things about how Jacob solved problems and worked with peers (additional advantages to sometimes taking the time to watch children closely), I knew that I could talk with Jacob about what he had done.

As their block building started to wind down, I asked Jacob if he could talk with me about what he had just done. At first he said, "I was building stuff with Heather." That led into a conversation about what exactly had happened first, second, and so on. From time to time I would ask questions as if I couldn't quite remember what had happened next, and Jacob was happy to fill in the details. After talking for a while I asked Jacob if he could write about building with blocks. Jacob was a bit hesitant, saying, "I don't think I can remember all of the parts." I told him he didn't need to remember everything and that I could help him with the book if he wanted. Once he got over the initial hurdle, he actually needed very little help. We simply talked about what might go on each page, with no expectation on my part that his book would end up the way we planned. We talked for a bit about how he could draw himself and Heather. After a few minutes Jacob's book was finished. (See Figure 6.3 on page 102.) Jacob's book is a good example of a book in which the value goes well beyond the finished product. Jacob was very proud of his book. It represented a step for him toward developing an image of himself as a writer, and it provided him with one strategy for finding a writing topic.

Connecting Oral Storytelling in Grades K–1 with Writing

For children in kindergarten and first grade, writing about experiences becomes a bit easier as children are able to more easily remember and sequence events. However, the more teachers expect children to be planning out their stories in advance of writing, the more support they will need. They also need additional support as teachers raise the expectations for how closely their finished product will match their initial ideas about the sequence of their book.

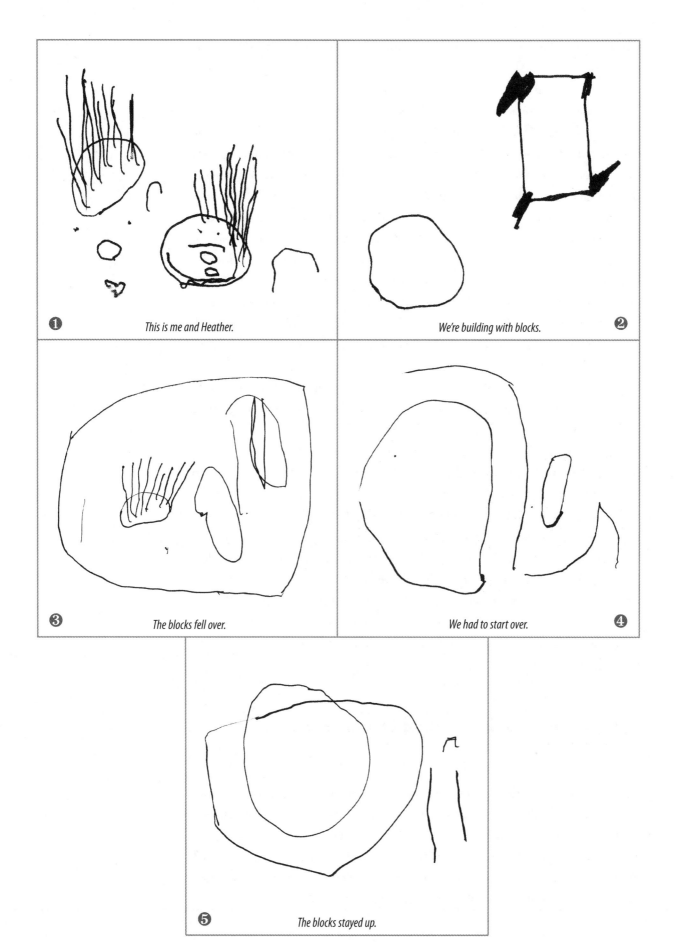

FIG. 6.3 *Jacob's Book About Block Building*

One useful strategy we can teach children to support their story sequencing is to practice telling their stories aloud before writing them. For many preschoolers, books are created as they go, which is developmentally appropriate for three-, four-, and some five-year-olds. With preschoolers, teachers aren't as concerned about children having their stories planned out in advance. But as children move into kindergarten they become more able to think about a story before writing. The most effective type of prewriting students can do is to tell their stories aloud to a teacher or a friend.

Students in preschool, kindergarten, and first grade should have regular time in the day to practice telling stories to each other. This form of oral rehearsal helps students in several ways. First, it helps them concentrate on only one thing by allowing them to think only about the story itself and not have to think about how to write the words or what to include in the illustrations. During an oral telling the child can focus on remembering the details of what happened, which for young children is sometimes enough of a challenge. Telling their story orally also helps in that they actually *hear* their story. Hearing themselves tell their story helps them figure out how their story should sound, which is harder for them to do if they are doing all of this work in their head. This also helps them figure out how to make it sound like a story instead of sounding like their everyday talk. Finally, oral storytelling helps them play around with the details of their story and to do some revision before writing.

In the same way, graphic organizers such as webs that are appropriate for intermediate-grade students aren't particularly effective for young children. For young children, a blank book is a more effective graphic organizer. With support, students can learn to tell their stories orally by saying what will go on each page. Telling their stories across blank pages adds one piece of the writing equation by adding in the element of planning out what will go on a page, a structure that may not be present when the child is simply telling a story orally.

After students have told a story orally and told it across blank pages, it will be easier to write on paper. Even then, it is not unusual or concerning for these stories to change as a child writes or for the written story to be different than it was told originally. Sometimes this represents actual revision, and sometimes it simply means that the child doesn't remember what she originally said. Either way, teachers should realize that students' stories will become more consistently linked to their oral retellings with experience, and they should be cautious of providing too much support to keep a story on track. If a teacher is providing a lot of support, then the balance of ownership for the story shifts from student to teacher and it becomes easy to inadvertently communicate that a student's approximations aren't good enough. We should always be aware of the intended and unintended messages we are sending children.

There is more to say about the subject of oral storytelling and talking in writing than I have room for here. For more information on the important role of oral storytelling for young writers, see *Talking, Drawing, Writing* (Horn and Giacobbe 2007) as well as the works of Vivian Paley (e.g., Paley 1990), a pioneer in understanding the value of children telling their own stories. While reading these resources and others, it is important to remember that telling personal stories is only one of many entry points into writing, and for some children it will not be the entry point with the most energy. You can also learn more about supporting personal narrative writing in Stephanie Parsons' book *First Grade Writers* (2005) and *Small Moments: Personal Narrative Writing* (Calkins and Oxenhorn 2003).

A Reminder and a Caution

As I mentioned in Chapter 2, teachers should be careful to make sure that students don't think that writing from experience is the only kind of writing they can do. Ultimately there should be a balance in the kinds of writing students are engaging in over the course of the year.

There is a potential downside to children constantly being on the prowl for book topics from things they see or do. Our friend's son Luke was in our daughters' preschool, a school where children are used to thinking like writers who are on the lookout for book ideas. One evening at bedtime Luke and his mother were talking and being silly and having a great time. As the conversation turned more and more silly, Luke's mother told a family story that, while funny, was also somewhat embarrassing. As Luke rolled with laughter, he said, "I'm going to write about that at school tomorrow." Luke's mother had to do some quick talking to avoid having this story become the topic of the next day's book sharing time at preschool.

That's exactly how we want young writers to think, even at the risk of embarrassing their parents.

Interest Entry Points

Writing About Passions

In the spring one of the teachers brought caterpillars into her preschool class. During their morning meeting the students examined the caterpillars and shared their many theories about how and when the caterpillars might turn into butterflies. Toward the end of the discussion the teacher asked the students where in the room they should put the caterpillars so they could continue to observe them. They knew they couldn't put the caterpillars in the sunlight or in front of the air vent, so they started to think about where they could go. Typical suggestions might have been in the science center, where there were other items related to nature, or on the large table in the classroom, where many students could observe them with magnify glasses. But not in this class. Right away Blake said, "We should put them in the writing center so that we can write books about them when they grow." This idea made perfect sense to the other children, so into the writing center went the caterpillars. Children did make books about the caterpillars, including Blake, whose book you can see in Figure 7.1 on page 106.

Blake had worked on this book independently over the course of several days. When asked about how he had decided to make this book, he said, in a very four-year-old way, "I know a lot of animals. Any sorts of animals. Caterpillars and gorillas and any sort of animals you want." Blake saw himself as an animal expert and an author, so writing about caterpillars was something natural and energizing for him.

There are some significant things to note about this interaction between Blake, his teacher, and his fellow students:

@ While Blake was not necessarily a reluctant writer, writing wasn't always Blake's first choice in the classroom. Blake was someone who liked to *tell*

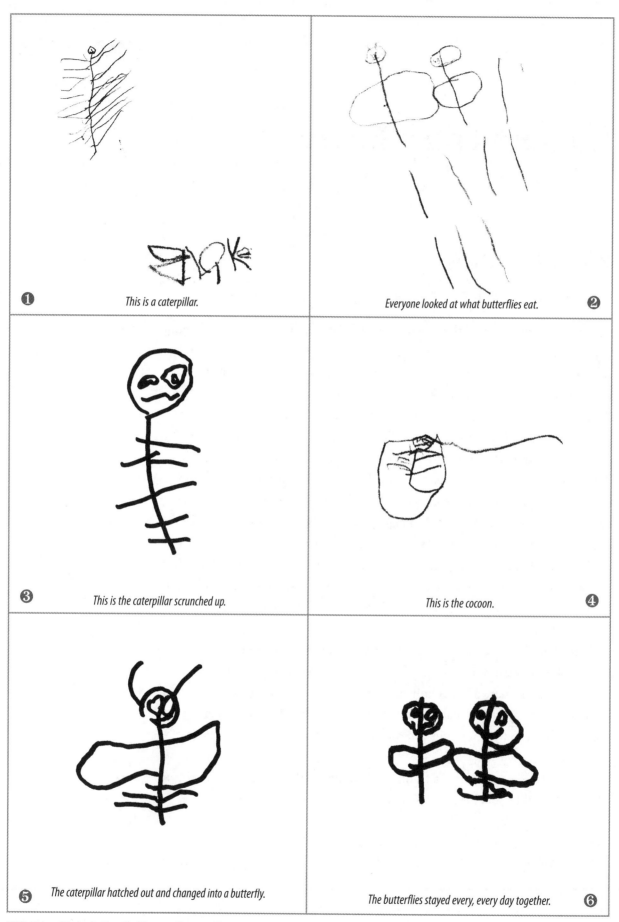

① This is a caterpillar.

② Everyone looked at what butterflies eat.

③ This is the caterpillar scrunched up.

④ This is the cocoon.

⑤ The caterpillar hatched out and changed into a butterfly.

⑥ The butterflies stayed every, every day together.

FIG. 7.1 **Blake's Book About Caterpillars**

stories, and stories were important to him. He was also interested in animals and things related to nature. So when he had an opportunity to combine his interests in stories and in nature, he had a different kind of energy and motivation for the writing process.

@ In this class, students were used to having opportunities to write about nature, science, and the world they observed each day. This book could have just as easily been about fossils, or leaves, or baby chicks.

@ In this classroom context, it made perfect sense for the caterpillars to go in the writing center, even though the teacher had made room for them in the science center. If she hadn't asked the children where the caterpillars should be placed, she wouldn't have learned as much about her students' connections between science and writing.

For many students, writing list books about topics they know a lot about or have interest in provides a meaningful entry point into writing. For some writers, entry points based on topics of interest provide a level of energy for the writing process that isn't present with other kinds of writing. Nonfiction writing simply seems to capture students, especially students who have little interest or energy for writing. I have frequently seen preschool, kindergarten, and first-grade students' attitudes about writing change for the better when they have started writing nonfiction. It makes sense, since if you know a lot about something, you are more motivated to write about it, and if you are interested enough to learn a lot about something, then you probably want to share your knowledge and interest with others.

The Importance of List Books and Nonfiction Writing

Most of the writing we do as adults is connected to nonfiction. Some of us may write poems or short stories or even write for a living, but the writing most of us do in the context of daily life is nonfiction. Newsletters, reports, even books about teaching young children about writing are nonfiction in nature.

Earlier we talked about the terms *storybooks* and *list books*: how storybooks could be fiction (made up) or nonfiction (true), and how list books could tell a lot about a topic or teach someone about a topic depending upon the author's intention. Nonfiction books can have parts that are written as narrative. For example, while there have been points in this book when I have shared narrative stories to illustrate ideas, this book will definitely end up in the nonfiction section of a library. While this chapter focuses on list books, we'll call this type of writing nonfiction, given that most teachers refer to books and children's writing that have the intent to share information on a topic as nonfiction writing.

We also know that many children gravitate toward nonfiction books, despite the fact that many of the books that are read during read-aloud in typical preschool, kindergarten, and first-grade classrooms are storybooks. If you watch a class of young children go to the school library, there is always a group of children who are continually drawn to the nonfiction section. Some kids check out every book on favorite topics, like cats or trains, while others simply browse the section looking for topics of interest. Often they select books that far exceed their reading level, in part because so much can be learned from the illustrations. Many of these children will spend their whole year in the nonfiction section and never venture over to the stories that are often read aloud in the classroom.

Despite many children's natural interest in nonfiction writing, much of their writing instruction throughout the year focuses on other types of writing. Like poetry, nonfiction writing usually takes place in a separate unit of study. Certainly nonfiction writing deserves to be focused on and studied closely. But if teachers want to capitalize on student energy for nonfiction writing, they should consider ways of supporting nonfiction writing throughout the year. Some of the ideas from Chapter 4, such as open units of study, provide opportunities for students who are drawn toward nonfiction writing to follow their passion.

Young Experts

Many children know a lot about certain topics. Recently a visitor to our school sat down next to a preschool student who was working on a book. Before the visitor could start talking to the child, he looked at her and said, "You know, I'm an expert on jet planes." He then proceeded to prove just how much he knew about jet planes. He quickly proved that he was an expert on jet planes, at least in the world of four-year-olds.

In early childhood classrooms children often develop identities as being experts on certain topics. Students in the classroom quickly figure out whom they should go to if they want to learn about insects, or pumpkins, or princesses, or jet planes. I'm constantly amazed at children who know much more about dinosaurs or birds than I do. I'm even more amazed when they know about more unusual topics that I never even considered becoming an expert on, like the preschool student who was an expert on John Deere tractors. John Deere tractor knowledge may not be a common topic on the playground at recess, but teachers can certainly capitalize on such an interest through writing.

Topic Choice

When children know a lot about a topic, that topic is a prime candidate for becoming a book. Not only do children who are experts on a topic have a ready store of information to put in their book, but they also have a built-in motivation to write about it. If children have a passion, then it is natural for them to want to write about it.

Sometimes children are passionate about topics that we might not be as eager for them to write about, such as battles and violence. Educators often struggle with the question of how to handle situations where children want to write about cartoons and movies. Topic choice can be particularly important for boy writers. In his book *Boy Writers: Reclaiming Their Voices*, Ralph Fletcher (2006) says, "Topic choice is one of the things that first drew me to the field of process writing. *Kids choose what they want to write about.* This fundamental, democratic tenet of the writing workshop appealed to me on many different levels. It made sense to me as a writer, and I could see how it resonated with young writers." Fletcher goes on to say, "But today for boys, it's not that simple. Many boys find that the 'choice coupon' in the writing workshop contains a great deal of small print listing many types of writing they are not allowed to do" (42). If our goal is to support energy for writing, then we must consider our own thoughts on topic choice.

Teachers often feel much more comfortable when a child who is passionate about fossils decides to write a book that teaches his friends about fossils than when a student who is passionate about Pokémon decides to write a book all about Pokémon. But, if we are going for energy and motivation, we need to be careful not to privilege one child's passion over another's simply because it may not match up with our vision of desirable topics.

When students choose topics that aren't the teacher's personal favorites or are concerning to him in some way, there are at least several choices he might make:

@ The teacher can encourage the child to write in a different way about the same topic. For example, for a student who is writing yet another Spider-Man adventure story, you might suggest he try writing a book on how to fight crime.

@ The teacher can gently nudge children toward different topics with suggestions at other times during the day. This book provides numerous examples of ways to help students find writing topics. By making suggestions about potential topics at other times, we can avoid stomping on a student's topic yet help her begin to see other writing possibilities. Some students have not spent considerable time thinking about topics or have not had meaningful support in finding topics. It's not surprising that these children rely on topics they know well. In general, if they are provided with attractive alternatives, coupled with topic-finding strategies, students will write on a variety of topics.

@ The teacher can simply allow students to write about topics that may not be the teacher's desired type of topic, supporting the students' motivation for writing about topics of their own interest.

@ The teacher can ban certain topics, especially ones that are unkind to other students or cross his line for being too violent. Some of those decisions are easy ones, but most fall into that gray area between student interest and teacher comfort. When making a decision to eliminate a topic, the teacher must make sure that what is gained (a more desirable topic) is worth what is potentially given up (energy for writing).

Ultimately teachers will make the decision about how to handle these topics. Often decisions are made on a case-by-case basis. While I obviously lean toward privileging energy for writing over teacher-directed topics, I encourage teachers to carefully consider their goals for writers when thinking about issues related to acceptable topics.

Nurturing Experts

What about children who don't think they are experts on any topics? It seems that we have more and more children in school who don't immediately appear to be curious, who don't ask questions constantly. One thing to consider is that these children likely know a lot of information about some topics, just not the ones that are typically found and valued in early childhood in classrooms. One of our first-grade students was an expert on feeding babies, something she did frequently at her house, where she was helping her single mother care for several siblings. This topic was every bit as valuable (and certainly more relevant to this student) than some typical writing topics. It is important that we communicate to students that typical school writing topics are not the only topics that are accepted and valued.

For children who don't appear to be curious, it is important that they have opportunities to become immersed in a topic, to hear children ask questions, and to ponder a problem over a long period of time. These are the children who most need experiences like studying a creek, as described in Chapter 3. Some of the most interesting and creative solutions and ideas during the creek investigation came from children with the least amount of the type of knowledge that is often valued in traditional classrooms. Some weren't the strongest readers or writers, but they used high levels of thinking to generate unique solutions to problems. In-depth learning experiences can provide opportunities for students to surpass their teachers' expectations.

Nonfiction writing can cut across differences between students. It doesn't require previous expertise in an area. The children in the preschool class who were interested in the butterflies all had an equal opportunity to write about them. They didn't rely on any previous knowledge about butterflies. Everyone could study butterflies, and everyone could write about them.

Furthermore, if we are careful to privilege expertise not only in certain topics but in all topics of interest, then we widen the possibility that nonfiction will appeal to students. Spider-Man or a TV show may not be what teachers would like for students to be experts in, but if our goal is to build on student energy as a way of encouraging writing, then we may need to use an inclusive definition of expert.

When children write about topics of interest, they write with a deeper level of investment because they have something they want to say. Fadhil, a kindergartner, showed this type of determination as he tried to teach his friends about the difference between whales and fish (see Figure 7.2 on page 112).

As you read his book you can quickly tell what Fadhil knows about how nonfiction writing works. He knows he can use dialogue in the illustrations to add some fun to his book. ("'Hi. I'm a mammal.' 'Hi. I am too.'"). He knows that the illustrations can emphasize a point from the text, as when he shows how big a whale is. He knows that he can ask his reader a question, as he does when he writes, "Whales are mammals like people. Aren't they? Yes! Or no. . . ."

You also learn that Fadhil wants to make sure his reader really knows that whales are mammals, not fish. One of the remarkable parts of Fadhil's book is his Flip-o-Rama page. To get the full effect of this feature, you would need to see what would happen when you flipped page 8 back and forth. Combined with the whale on page 9, with its tale in the up position, you'd see the whale's tail appear to move up and down (not side to side like a fish). I asked Fadhil how he had figured out how to make the whale's tail move up and down, thinking that he probably had a whale book that worked like this and had re-created it, which would have been impressive enough. Instead, Fadhil replied, "I have a book at home with a giant and when you flip the page like that, he stomps up and down. So I thought I could do the same thing with the whale's tale." Fadhil took what he knew about nonfiction writing and what he had noticed as he read like a writer to clearly illustrate his point about the difference between whales and fish.

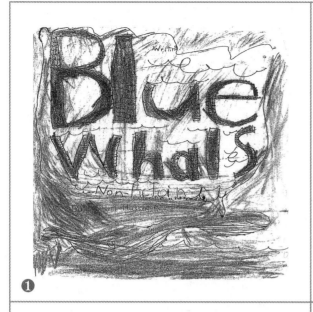

①

for my freind James Ulmer

②

They're as big as This

Blue whals are the Bigest whales in the world. they are. as too big Houses. they are blue. that's why they're called blue whals they're Gigantic!

Blue whales are the biggest whales in the world. They are as too big houses. They are blue. That's why they're called blue whales. They're gigantic!

③

Whales are mamals like peaple.

Hi I'm a Mammal.
Hi I am To.

Arnt they? yes!
Or No...
Some peaple think that whales are fish. But they're... Not! the only Diffren is whales can't Beath under water.

Whales are mammals like people. Aren't they? Yes! Or no.... Some people think that whales are fish. But they're ... not! The only difference is whales can't breath under water.

④

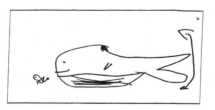

But fish can. Becuase whales are mammals. Not fish! whales move they're Tails up and town. not side to side like fish Flip-O-rama next Page

But fish can. Because whales are mammals. Not fish! Whales move their tails up and down, not side to side like fish. Flip-o-Rama next page.

⑤

FIG. 7.2 *Fadhil's Book About Blue Whales*

⑥ Flip o Rama

Hold the Book Flat
AND Flip
The pages.

⑦ LeFt Hand Here

⑧

⑨ Fish move they're tails side to side not Ug and down like whales do. Fish are not mammals.

Fish move their tails side to side, not up and down like whales do. Fish are not mammals.

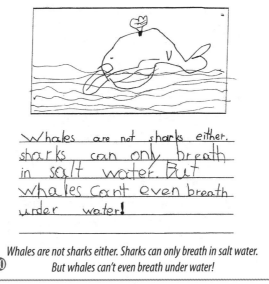

⑩ Whales are not sharks either. sharks can only breath in salt water. But whales can't even breath under water!

Whales are not sharks either. Sharks can only breath in salt water. But whales can't even breath under water!

FIG. 7.2 *(continued)*

What's more significant is that if Fadhil weren't in a class where children made books and studied nonfiction writing closely, this book would never have been created and his teacher would have missed out on the sophisticated thinking he could do at age six. Before students at our school started studying writing closely and making books, we had students like Fadhil who didn't have the opportunity to show what they could do.

We frequently say we're surprised by the latest interesting insight a child has made, which makes us wonder how many surprises are inside children each day, waiting to be discovered.

Understanding the Difference Between Storybooks and List Books

Helping young children understand the difference between storybooks and list books isn't always easy. Teachers often talk about list books and nonfiction books as interchangeable. But what teachers typically think of as nonfiction books are actually a particular type of list book (remember, storybooks are nonfiction too when the story is true).

When I refer to nonfiction books here, I'm talking about books in which the author has the intention of doing one of several things:

- Teach people about a topic. Most typical nonfiction writing provides a lot of information that helps a reader learn about a topic.

- Teach people specifically how to do something.

- Write about a topic with the intention of both engaging and informing the reader about the topic. This goes beyond just teaching information about a topic since information is presented in a way that is interesting to read. This type of writing is called literary nonfiction (Ray and Cleaveland 2004, 192).

List books can also just tell a lot about a topic. A book like Tate's book about his friends in his preschool class is a list book (see Figure 7.3). It's technically nonfiction since it is true (Logan really does like spaceships), but Tate's purpose isn't to teach you about his friends or to engage and inform you. His purpose is simply to tell you one thing about each of his friends, and he does it in the format of a list book.

One of our goals with very young children is to help them understand the difference between nonfiction books and other types of books. We want children to be thinking about an audience as they write. They need to be deciding on a

FIG. 7.3 **Tate's Book About His Friends**

purpose for writing. Audience and purpose are big ideas for any writer, so we expect young, less experienced writers to do this in approximated ways. But if we are willing to honor these approximations, we can start talking with children about how different kinds of books have different purposes and audiences.

We can help children start to see these differences by simply talking with them about the books they are reading as a class. Teachers can talk with children about the authors' purposes in writing. Some inform, some share a memory, some entertain, some simply share about something they love, and some teach facts about a topic.

As children start to understand the differences in purpose they can start to try this out in their own writing. In Kyle's kindergarten class his teacher knew that she was getting ready to start a unit of study on nonfiction writing. One day she was conferring with Kyle about a book he had written about going fishing with his grandfather. They talked for a bit about his book and what a good time he'd had fishing with his grandfather. As they talked about the kind of fish they'd caught it became apparent that Kyle knew a lot about fishing, so she decided to see if he could also write a nonfiction fishing book. She said, "Kyle, this is really interesting how you told the story of going fishing with your grandfather. I was wondering if you might also be able to write a book that would teach people what you know about fishing. Maybe it would tell people how to fish, or maybe it would just tell a lot about fish and fishing. Do you want to try that?"

Being the agreeable kid that he was, Kyle decided to give it a try. Figure 7.4 shows his original storybook, and Figure 7.5 shows Kyle's list/nonfiction book. While it doesn't teach you about *how* to fish, it does show some of what Kyle knows about fish. More importantly it clearly shows that Kyle understands the fundamental difference between story writing and nonfiction writing. In his first book he is writing about an experience and in his second book he is writing to teach you a bit about fish.

Kyle's teacher used his books as she launched the class study of nonfiction. She had pairs of books about similar topics that the class had read earlier in the year, one storybook and one list book for each topic. The students looked at similarities and differences in the kinds of books. After talking about a couple of published books, the teacher came to Kyle's fish books and read them to the students. They discussed these just like the other published authors but now had the clear advantage of being able to interview the author in person. The teacher and students asked Kyle about how he had made his books. Kyle soon became the resident nonfiction expert.

Literary Nonfiction

If Kyle read some literary nonfiction it probably wouldn't be too much of a stretch for him to try to inform and engage his reader all in one book. Meredith, a first grader, did just that in her book about the balance beam. Her class had been reading a large stack of literary nonfiction, including books like *Atlantic*, by Brian Karas (2004), and *Tiger Trail*, by Karen Winters (2000), that are written in first person from the perspective of the subject of the book—in these books, from the perspective of the Atlantic Ocean and a tiger, respectively.

After reading these books Meredith was inspired to try this technique on her own. Meredith was an enthusiastic gymnast. She had written other books about gymnastics, usually storybooks about specific gymnastics experiences. She decided with this new gymnastics book to try something different and write from the perspective of the balance beam. You can see in Figure 7.6 on page 120, that she

FIG. 7.4 **Kyle's Fishing Story**

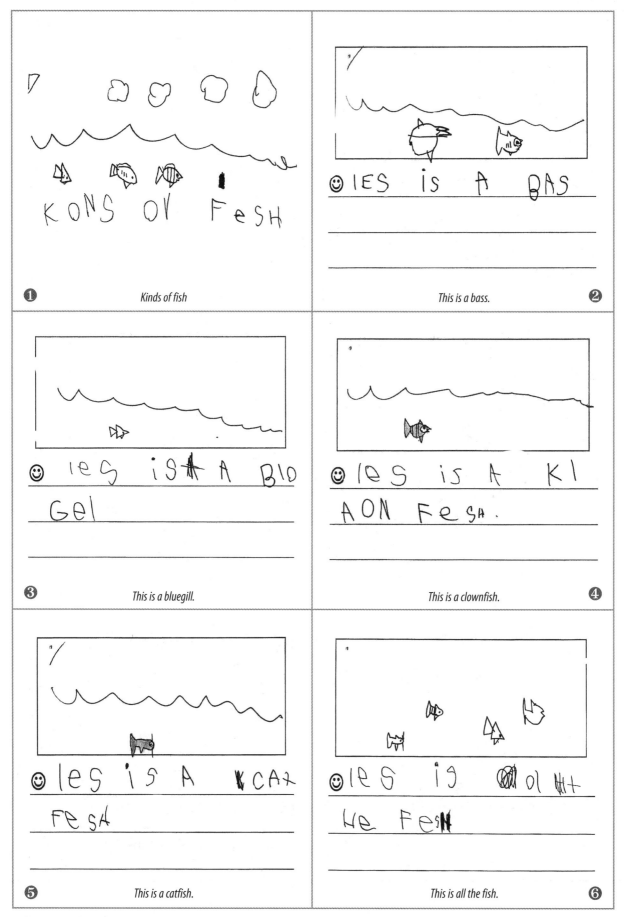

FIG. 7.5 *Kyle's Fishing List Book*

succeeded. The last page shows that she truly understands writing from another perspective as she switches from writing in first person in her author's note to writing from the perspective of the beam in the "Facts About the Beam" section.

Teddy, also a first grader, tried this same thing in his book about trees. His first-grade class read many of the same books that Meredith's class read, but you can see how Teddy included more of a narrative structure in his book. As often happens with some young writers, the narrative portion took over. His work on this book stretched over several weeks, and it ended up more than thirty pages long. I've included only a few pages here. Teddy told the story from the perspective of the tree throughout the entire book. (See Figure 7.7 on page 122.)

Writing from the perspective of their topic is just one of the ways authors can engage and inform at the same time. A few of the other ways are

- embedding facts in illustrations, like Nicola Davies does in her books;

- including a page at the end that shares facts about the topic, like in *Red Eyed Tree Frog* (Cowley 1999) or *An Island Grows* (Schaefer 2006); or

- structuring the books as a series of questions and answers, as in *Do I Bug You?* (Moog 2006).

For more detailed information on literary nonfiction, see *About the Authors*, by Katie Ray and Lisa Cleaveland (2004, 192).

How-to Writing

Another type of nonfiction writing is books that teach a reader how to do something. There are few picture books that are entirely devoted to teaching how to do one thing, although there are some. *Walk On!* by Marla Frazee (2006) is ideal in that it includes many of the elements of this type of writing—including the specific sequence of what to do, tips on how to be successful at what you're trying, and cautions about potential difficulties. It also shows that you can write about common, everyday accomplishments, like learning to walk. It's a book that preschool children relate to well.

Teachers who haven't been thinking a lot about writing in preschool might not think of how-to writing as a possible genre for preschool children. But if teachers are willing to accept preschoolers' approximations (that they will write how-to books the way a four-year-old would write a how-to book), young children can certainly write this way.

One day in preschool I watched a first-year teacher and a group of students carve a pumpkin. They had decided what it should look like and had all helped

1 — I Am the Beam!

2 — I am the beam. People jump and twist on me. Twirl and fall on me?

3 — People do danger on me!

4 — People love to go on me.

5 — I love me. I am creative and fun.

6 — You can just walk across me!

FIG. 7.6 **Meredith's Book About the Balance Beam**

You can dow anething oh me.

❼ *You can do anything on me.*

You can dow hafi to got oh me a Shtit way!

You have to get on me a certain way! ❽

You can dow ohe Sot uv chik oh me.

❾ *You can do any sort of trick on me.*

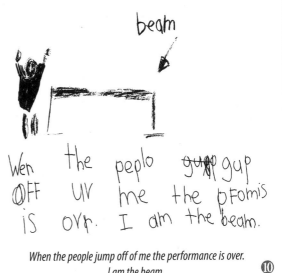

beam

Wen the peplo gup OFF uv me the pfomis is ovr. I am the beam.

*When the people jump off of me the performance is over.
I am the beam.* ❿

About the Author

I did this book to teach kids about the balance beam. I think the balance beam is neat and cool. The balance beam is one of my favorite things about gymnastics. I thought of this book because we read *Atlantic*.

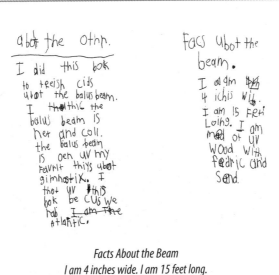

abot the othn.

I did this bok to teeish cids ubot the balus beam. I thit this the balus beam is net and coll. the balus beam is oen uv my favrit thiys ubot gimhastix. I thot uv this bok be cus we rab I am the Atlantic.

Facs ubot the beam.

I adm 4 ichis wib. I am 15 feti loihg. I am med ot uv wood with fedric and send.

❶❶

*Facts About the Beam
I am 4 inches wide. I am 15 feet long.
I am made of wood with fabric and sand.*

FIG. 7.6 *(continued)*

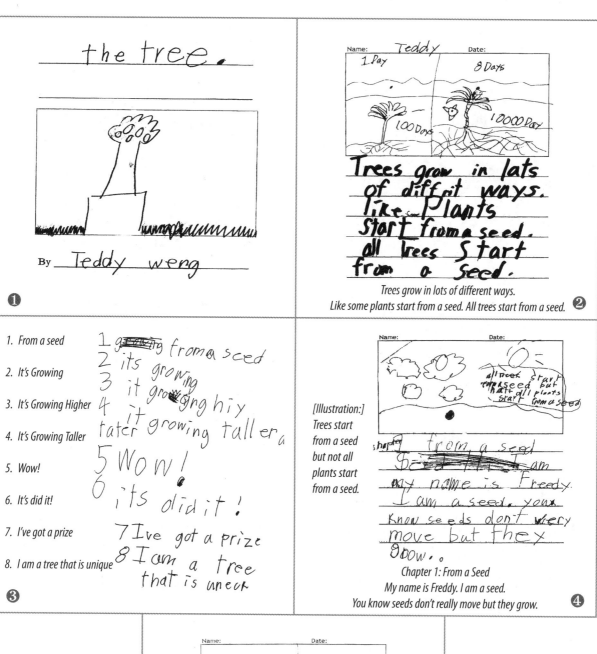

①

the tree.

By Teddy weng

②

Name: Teddy   Date:

1. Day   8 Days
100 Days   10000 Day

Trees grow in lats
of diffrit ways.
Like some Plants
start from a seed.
all trees start
from a seed.

Trees grow in lots of different ways.
Like some plants start from a seed. All trees start from a seed.

③

1. From a seed
2. It's Growing
3. It's Growing Higher
4. It's Growing Taller
5. Wow!
6. It's did it!
7. I've got a prize
8. I am a tree that is unique

1 g̶e̶t̶t̶i̶n̶g̶ from a seed
2 its growing
3 it growing hiy
4 tater growing taller a
5 Wow!
6 its did it!
7 Ive got a prize
8 I am a tree
that is uneck

④

Name: Date:

all trees start
from a seed but
natt all plants
start from a seed

[Illustration:]
Trees start
from a seed
but not all
plants start
from a seed.

chapter from a seed
Seed I am
my name is Freddy.
I am a seed. you
know seeds don't very
move but they
grow.

Chapter 1: From a Seed
My name is Freddy. I am a seed.
You know seeds don't really move but they grow.

⑤

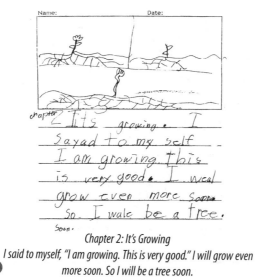

Name: Date:

chapter 2 Its growing. I
sayad to my self
I am growing. this
is very good. I weal
grow even more soon
So. I wale be a tree.
Soon.

Chapter 2: It's Growing
I said to myself, "I am growing. This is very good." I will grow even
more soon. So I will be a tree soon.

FIG. 7.7 **Excerpts from Teddy's Book About Trees**

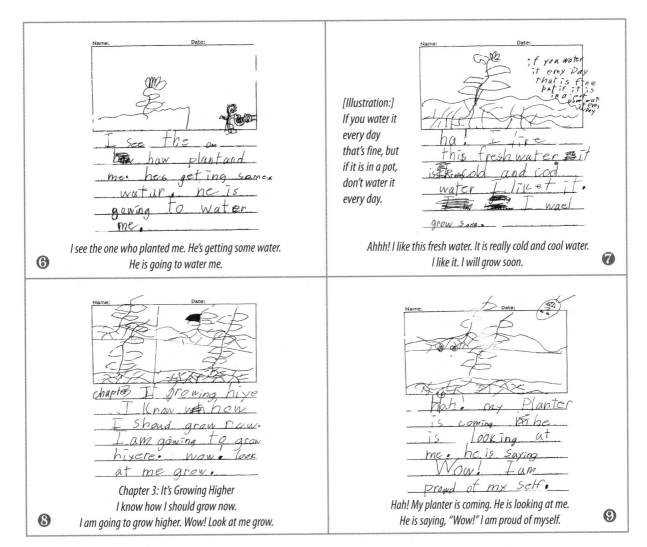

I see the one who planted me. He's getting some water.
He is going to water me.

❻

[Illustration:]
If you water it
every day
that's fine, but
if it is in a pot,
don't water it
every day.

Ahhh! I like this fresh water. It is really cold and cool water.
I like it. I will grow soon.

❼

Chapter 3: It's Growing Higher
I know how I should grow now.
I am going to grow higher. Wow! Look at me grow.

❽

Hah! My planter is coming. He is looking at me.
He is saying, "Wow!" I am proud of myself.

❾

FIG. 7.7 **(continued)**

scoop out the pumpkin guts. As I watched all of this I wondered if the teacher
would make the suggestion to the children that they might decide to make a
book about what they did or how to carve a pumpkin. Even though students frequently made books in her class, I wasn't surprised that she missed this opportunity to suggest that someone might make a book about this experience. But I
couldn't help myself, so as they were getting ready to go off and do something else,
I asked them to stay for a minute. I asked them about the steps they had followed
to carve the pumpkin and then asked them if they were going to make a book,
what they would put on the first page, and so on. I got very few answers to any
of my questions and there was little interest in my conversation. After a couple
of minutes it was clear that the kids were close to revolting, so I let them go.

I had clearly chosen the worst possible time to talk about how they could write
a book. They had been there for a while, the pumpkin was finished, and so were

they. There were at least two much better options. One would have been to have talked with them while they were carving the pumpkin, saying things like, "If you were going to make a book about carving a pumpkin, what would you put on the first page?" This is similar to what you might hear a teacher say as she talks with students about the steps of carving a pumpkin as they are doing it. Adding the simple twist of putting this conversation in book language could have supported later pumpkin-carving books.

Another option would have been to bring the idea up later at circle time at the end of the morning or the next day as a way of revisiting the pumpkin-carving experience. This way all of the students in the class could have heard the suggestion "You could make a book that teaches people about carving a pumpkin."

But, even with my poorly timed teaching move, Elliot did make a book about carving a pumpkin on his own. After he left the pumpkin-carving table, Elliot popped in on a couple of different centers but didn't stay long. After a bit he went over to the writing area and got a piece of paper and drew a picture. He walked over to me and showed me his picture. I asked, "Is that a picture?" since I wasn't sure if it was a picture or a book or a letter.

Elliot replied, "Yes. You know, I'm an artist."

I told him he certainly was, and that I knew he was an author, too, and reminded him that I had seen him make a book earlier that week. He agreed, and then without prompting went back to the writing center. From across the room I saw him get a blank book and start working on it. A few minutes later he came back with his book. He told me it was a book about how to carve a pumpkin. After he read it to me, I went back and asked him more about the page where the top of the pumpkin was cut off. I asked if one of the objects was a knife, and he said no. So I asked him if he was going to add a knife, and he said, "No, I can't draw a knife," which was interesting since he had just talked about being an artist. So we talked for a bit about how he could draw a knife and I assured him that I thought he could draw one. He went back over to the writing center and a minute later came back and showed me the knife he had added to the page. (See Figure 7.8.)

Even an ill-timed teaching move about a possible book topic resulted in Elliot deciding to initiate making a book. A large reason for this was that his classroom environment was one where children made books on a regular basis. This teacher chose better times during the day to frequently suggest book topics and children were used to acting upon those suggestions.

For Elliot, writing about something he knew how to do was a particularly good entry point into writing. For someone else in this class, writing might have been sparked if I had asked if the students thought they'd see pumpkins when they

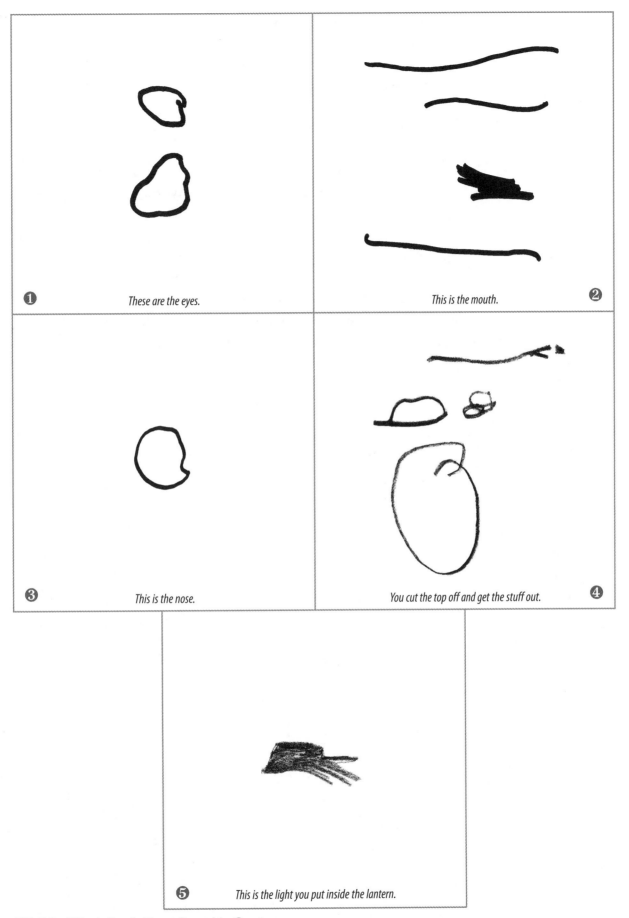

FIG. 7.8 **Elliot's Book About Pumpkin Carving**

went trick-or-treating, which could have led to them writing a storybook about going trick-or-treating. The more we know about students, the better we can help match students with entry points into writing.

The Power of Interest

Perhaps more than any other entry point, writing about topics of interest, topics students know about, can entice students who are typically less energetic writers. As teachers we can't underestimate the motivating power of interest. When non-fiction writing is combined with the conceptual entry points of meaning, choice, and purpose, it becomes even more powerful. When children are writing about a topic that has meaning and interest to them, when they are choosing a topic they love rather than one that someone else loves, and when their books have an authentic purpose in the world, the quality of their writing (as well as their attitude toward writing) will exceed our expectations.

Final Thoughts

An Epilogue

Last spring the children in one of our preschool classes became interested in epilogues. Understanding epilogues doesn't appear in any of our state standards or local curriculum. It's also not the kind of thing preschool teachers usually decide to teach. But the preschool students in this class were used to noticing what writers do in their books, and they had a teacher who nurtured their questions and interests. So when they read *Knuffle Bunny Too* (Willems 2007), they became interested in the epilogue at the end of the book that shows Trixie and Sonja at school the day after they switched their bunnies. As they reread the book they became more and more interested in the epilogue and wondered if other books had them too. They checked the books in their class, and each week when they went to the library, they turned to the backs of their newly selected books to see if an epilogue was waiting.

After I heard about this unusual interest, I asked one of the children what an epilogue was. She said, "A catalog [as they sometimes misnamed *epilogue*] is a part of the book that comes after the story is over and tells you a little more about the story." A pretty good definition. Elliot, one of the children in the class, became so interested in epilogues that he and some of his friends decided to write their own epilogues for one of their favorite books, *The Three Billy Goats Gruff*, by Paul Galdone (1981). In this version they noticed the fish in the river and wondered what happened to the troll after he fell off the bridge. In Elliot's epilogue (see Figure 8.1) you can see that the troll is eaten by the fish, putting a more complete closure on the story, in Elliot's mind. Elliot's class stayed on the lookout for more epilogues in picture books. They eventually found one in *Chrysanthemum*, by Kevin Henkes (1991), and they continued looking for the rest of the year.

① *The troll fell into the water.*

② *The fish ate him.*

③ *Elliot*

FIG. 8.1 *Elliot's Epilogue*

Elliot's and his classmates' interest in epilogues showed that they knew that writers, young and old, learn from other authors. So I thought I'd take what I learned from Elliot and write a "little more" by sharing some recommendations.

One of the questions that always pops up from teachers is "What do I do next?" Here are some short-term ideas:

@ First and foremost, if your children aren't already making books, simply give them blank books and have them start making them. The shift from "I'm writing on a single page" to "I'm making a book" is a powerful one.

@ Look at each name on your class list and think about each student in terms of suitable entry points into writing. Write down which entry points might be the most inviting for each student.

@ If you don't know which entry points might fit best with each child, start thinking about what motivates individual children as you talk with them. What are their interests? Are they story players? What do they talk about? The more you know about them, the better you can invite them into writing.

@ Consider how you will start the year in your kindergarten or first-grade writing workshop. What are your goals for the first two months of writing? In light of those goals, consider trying one or more of the units described in Chapter 4 and read the suggested related resources as you plan these key early units.

@ List all of the other activities and situations during the school day that can relate to writing. When do children have an opportunity to play and how can you help them mine their play for story topics? What experiences do they have in school that they could write about? What are they really in-terested in, either individually or as a group, that they could write about? Looking at a typical day through a writing-topic lens can help you see new ideas.

@ Ensure that children have plenty of choice as they write. In kindergarten and first grade, make sure that there are opportunities throughout the year when they can choose the genre in which they are going to write, includ-ing genres they may not have studied previously.

@ What interactions do you have on a regular basis with your students in which you have a chance to just talk and learn more about them as indi-viduals? If there aren't many, consider how you can add a few brief oppor-tunities into each day.

@ Often teachers send a survey home to parents before the start of the year in which parents can share information about their child. Look at these surveys as a source of potential entry points into writing for students. Ques-tions such as "What is your child passionate about?" or "Does your child create stories through stories, play, or drawing?" are a good place to start.

Thinking about meaning, choice, and purpose isn't new to teaching in gen-eral or to the teaching of writing, but it is essential. The issues of meaning, choice, and purpose address deeply held beliefs about the role of the teacher, the role of the student, and what it means to truly learn. For example, a teacher's opinion about the balance of control in a classroom is often a deeply held belief. Altering such beliefs and actions is a gradual process. To support this thinking you might try the following:

- Take your lesson plans for the last week and look at the activities in which children were engaged. Look at each activity and ask: How meaningful was this activity to the child? What would a child say was the purpose of doing this activity? How deeply engaged were children with each experience? Every experience won't produce deep engagement, but some certainly should.

- Examine the role of choice in your classroom. Count how many meaningful choices children get to make each day.

- Read about children's intellectual growth. A short list to start with could include:
  - *To Understand* (Keene 2008)
  - *The Hundred Languages of Children* (Edwards, Gandini, and Forman 1998)
  - *Young Investigators* (Helm and Katz 2000)
  - *Research Workshop* (Rogovin 2001)
  - *Bringing Learning to Life* (Cadwell 2002)
  - *Constructivism Across the Curriculum in Early Childhood Classrooms* (Chaille 2007)
  - *Discovering and Exploring Habits of Mind* (Costa and Kallick 2000)

- Become an advocate for teacher decision making based on individual needs. Increasingly schools and educators are looking toward programs that make decisions for teachers. Deeply engaging, meaningful, and purposeful experiences can occur only when teachers make instructional decisions based on the interests and needs of the students in their class in a particular year.

Lilian Katz reminds us that one of the key questions educators might ask ourselves is: If I asked my students what I really think is important, what would they say? Would they say the teacher thinks it's important for us listen carefully and quietly to what she says? That we get the right answer? That we ask really good questions? It's a fundamental question: What do students think their teacher really values?

In our journey with young writers, I hope that students come to believe that their teachers care about fostering energy and passion for writing as much as how well children write. Fortunately, thoughtful teachers who think carefully about how they invite children to enter into writing will ensure that their students' first steps as writers, and the ones that follow, will lead to children who have images of themselves as powerful authors.

Appendix

Possible Entry Points for Young Writers

Here are the entry points all on one page. You can copy this and use it as a reminder when you're considering entry points into writing for young writers.

Essential Entry Points

- ℮ *Meaning*—Why is this book meaningful for a child?

- ℮ *Choice*—What choices did the child make?

- ℮ *Purpose*—What is the children's purpose for writing? Who is the audience?

Invitational Entry Points

- ℮ *Invitations through conversations*—preschool

- ℮ *Curriculum and units of study*—primary grades

Story Entry Points

- ℮ *Dramatic play*—writing that is sparked by children's dramatic play

- ℮ *Read-aloud*—writing that is sparked by books children know and love

Experience Entry Points

- ℮ *Writing sparked by children's experiences*

Interest Entry Points

- ℮ *List book (nonfiction) writing* sparked by a child's interest in a topic

References

Works Cited

Bennett-Armistead, V., N. Duke, and A. Moses. 2005. *Literacy and the Youngest Learner: Best Practices for Educators of Children from Birth to 5*. New York: Scholastic.

Berry, M. A. 2007. Conversation with the Creekside Early Childhood Study Group. Creekside Early Childhood School. West Chester, OH. November 16, 2007.

Bodrova, E., and D. Leong. 1996. *Tools of the Mind: The Vygotskian Approach to Early Childhood Education*. Englewood Cliffs, NJ: Prentice Hall.

Cadwell, L. 2002. *Bringing Learning to Life*. New York: Teachers College Press.

Calkins, L., and L. Mermelstein. 2003. *Launching the Writing Workshop*. Vol. 1, *Units of Study for Primary Writing: A Yearlong Curriculum*. Portsmouth, NH: firsthand, Heinemann.

Calkins, L., and A. Oxenhorn. 2003. *Small Moments: Personal Narrative Writing*. Vol. 2, *Units of Study for Primary Writing: A Yearlong Curriculum*. Portsmouth, NH: firsthand, Heinemann.

Chaille, C. 2007. *Constructivism Across the Curriculum in Early Childhood Classrooms: Big Ideas as Inspiration*. Boston: Allyn and Bacon.

Costa, A., and B. Kallick. 2000. *Discovering and Exploring Habits of Mind*. Arlington, VA: ASCD.

Edwards, C., L. Gandini, and G. Forman, eds. 1998. *The Hundred Languages of Children: The Reggio Emilia Approach—Advanced Reflections*. 2d ed. Westport, CT: Ablex.

Feynman, R. 1999. *The Pleasure of Finding Things Out: The Best Short Works of Richard Feynman*. Cambridge, MA: Helix Books.

Fletcher, R. 2006. *Boy Writers: Reclaiming Their Voices*. Portland, ME: Stenhouse.

Fletcher, R., and J. Portalupi. 2001. *Writing Workshop: The Essential Guide*. Portsmouth, NH: Heinemann.

Helm, J., and L. Katz. 2000. *Young Investigators: The Project Approach in the Early Years*. New York: Teachers College Press.

Horn, M., and M. E. Giacobbe. 2007. *Talking, Drawing, Writing: Lessons for Our Youngest Writers*. Portland, ME: Stenhouse.

Johnston, P. 2004. *Choice Words: How Our Language Affects Children's Learning*. Portland, ME: Stenhouse.

Jones, S. 2006. *Girls, Social Class and Literacy: What Teachers Can Do to Make a Difference*. Portsmouth, NH: Heinemann.

Katz, L. 1998. "What Can We Learn from Reggio Emilia?" In *The Hundred Languages of Children: The Reggio Emilia Approach—Advanced Reflections*, 2d ed., ed. C. Edwards, L. Gandini, and G. Forman, 27–45. Westport, CT: Ablex.

Keene, E. 2008. *To Understand: New Horizons in Reading Comprehension*. Portsmouth, NH: Heinemann.

Louis, N. 2008. Presentation, Teachers College Reading and Writing Project Saturday Reunion. Columbia University. New York, NY. March 29, 2008.

Neuman, S., and K. Roskos. 2007. *Nurturing Knowledge: Building a Foundation for School Success by Linking Early Literacy to Math, Science, Art, and Social Studies*. New York: Scholastic.

Newkirk, T. 1989. *More Than Stories: The Range of Children's Writing*. Portsmouth, NH: Heinemann.

Owocki, G. 1999. *Literacy Through Play*. Portsmouth, NH: Heinemann.

———. 2001. *Make Way for Literacy! Teaching the Way Young Children Learn*. Portsmouth, NH: Heinemann.

Paley, V. 1990. *The Boy Who Would Be a Helicopter*. Cambridge, MA: Harvard University Press.

Parsons, S. 2005. *First Grade Writers: Units of Study to Help Children Plan, Organize, and Structure Their Ideas*. Portsmouth, NH: Heinemann.

Ray, K. W. 2006. *Study Driven: A Framework for Planning Units of Study in the Writing Workshop*. Portsmouth, NH: Heinemann.

Ray, K. W., with L. Cleaveland. 2004. *About the Authors: Writing Workshop with Our Youngest Writers*. Portsmouth, NH: Heinemann.

Ray, K. W., and M. Glover. 2008. *Already Ready: Nurturing Writers in Preschool and Kindergarten*. Portsmouth, NH: Heinemann.

Rogovin, P. 2001. *Research Workshop: Bringing the World into Your Classroom*. Portsmouth, NH: Heinemann.

Schlechty, P. 1997. *Inventing Better Schools: An Action Plan for Educational Reform*. San Francisco, CA: Jossey-Bass.

Picture Books

Cowley, J. 1999. *Red Eyed Tree Frog*. Photo. N. Bishop. New York: Scholastic.

Crews, D. 1985. *Freight Train*. New York: Puffin Books.

Davies, N. 2005. *One Tiny Turtle: Read and Wonder*. Cambridge, MA: Candlewick.

Fisher, V. 2002. *My Big Brother*. New York: Simon and Schuster

Frazee, M. 2006. *Walk On! A Guide for Babies of All Ages*. Orlando, FL: Harcourt.

French. J. 2003. *Too Many Pears!* Illus. B. Whatley. New York: Star Bright Books.

Galdone, P. 1981. *The Three Billy Goats Gruff*. New York: Clarion.

Gray, L. M. 1995. *My Mama Had a Dancing Heart*. New York: Orchard Books.

Henkes, K. 1991. *Chrysanthemum*. New York: Greenwillow Books.

———. 2000. *Wemberly Worried*. New York: Greenwillow Books.

Karas, B. 2004. *Atlantic*. New York: Puffin.

Lionni, L. 1994. *Little Blue and Little Yellow: A Story for Pippo and Other Children*. New York: Mulberry Books.

Marshall, J. 2000. *The Three Little Pigs*. New York: Penguin.

Moog, B. 2006. *Do I Bug You? A "Who Am I?" Book*. San Francisco: University Games.

Reynolds, P. H. 2004. *Ish*. Cambridge, MA: Candlewick.

Rosen, M. 1989. *Going on a Bear Hunt*. Illus. H. Oxenbury. London: Walker Books.

Schaefer, L. 2006. *An Island Grows*. Illus. C. Felstead. New York: Greenwillow Books.

Silverstein, S. 1981. *A Light in the Attic*. New York: Harper and Row.

Waddell, M. 1975. *Owl Babies*. Illus. P. Benson. Cambridge, MA: Candlewick.

Wallace, K. 2002. *Gentle Giant Octopus: Read and Wonder*. Illus. M. Bostock. Cambridge, MA: Candlewick.

Watt, M. 2006. *Scaredy Squirrel*. Tonawanda, NY: Kids Can.

Willems, M. 2004. *Knuffle Bunny*. New York. Hyperion.

———. 2007. *Knuffle Bunny Too*. New York: Hyperion.

Wilson, K. 2006. *Whopper Cake*. Illus. W. Hillenbrand. New York: Margaret K. McElderry Books.

Winters, K. 2000. *Tiger Trail*. Illus. Laura Regan. New York: Simon and Schuster.

Index

Paley, Vivian (*Boy Who Would Be a Helicopter, The*), 71, 104

paper, choice of, 43

parents, as indicator of deep engagement, 39–40

Parsons, Stephanie (*First Grade Writers: Units of Study to Help Children Plan, Organize, and Structure Their Ideas*), 62, 65, 104

passions, writing about. *See* interest entry points

play, dramatic. *See* dramatic play

Pleasure of Finding Things Out, The: The Best Short Works of Richard Feynman (Feynman), 36

Portalupi, JoAnn (*Writing Workshop: The Essential Guide*), 42, 44

pretend play. *See* dramatic play

prewriting discussions, 96

purpose
    as essential entry point, 35–37, 44–48, 129–30
    thinking about, while writing, 115

Ray, Katie W., vi–vii, 25, 57
    About the Authors: Writing Workshop with Our Youngest Writers, 62, 65, 114, 119
    Already Ready: Nurturing Writers in Preschool and Kindergarten (see *Already Ready: Nurturing Writers in Preschool and Kindergarten* (Ray & Glover))
    Study Driven: A Framework for Planning Units of Study in the Writing Workshop, 50

read-alouds
    favorite books (*see* favorite read-alouds)
    whole-group teaching within, 51

reading like writers
    as cutting across age groups, 50
    teaching children, 4, 13–14, 15
    unit of study, 61, 65

Red-Eyed Tree Frog (Cowley), 119

reluctant writers
    defined, 56
    invitational entry points for, 55–56

Research Workshop (Rogovin), 130

revision, in prewriting discussion, 96

Reynolds, Peter (*Ish*), 12

Rogovin, Paula (*Research Workshop*), 130

Rosen, Michael (*Going on a Bear Hunt*), 84

Roskos, Kathleen (*Nurturing Knowledge: Building a Foundation for School Success by Linking Early Literacy to Math, Science, Art, and Social Studies*), 71, 72

Schaefer, Lola M. (*Island Grows, An*), 119

Schlechty, Phillip C. (*Inventing Better Schools: An Action Plan for Educational Reform*), 40

sequencing
    in prewriting discussion, 96
    strategies for teaching, 103

share time, whole-group teaching with, 52

sharing, with dramatic play, 74

Silverstein, Shel (*Light in the Attic, A*), 9

small-group teaching in preschool and K–1 classes, compared, 52

Small Moments: Personal Narrative Writing. Vol. 2, Units of Study for Primary Writing: A Yearlong Curriculum (Calkins & Oxenhorn), 104

Star Wars, 80, 81

stories
    naming children's writing as, 26
    story writing, 27–28

storybooks
    as kind of writing for children, 25–26, 107
    and list books, understanding difference between, 114–16, 117–18

story entry points
    defined, 33
    dramatic play (*see* dramatic play)
    favorite books read-alouds (*see* favorite read-alouds)

storytelling
    maximizing student energy with, 66
    as oral rehearsal, 103
    value of, 27
    writing, connecting oral storytelling with, 101, 103–4

Strickland, Dorothy, 85

structures that support writing, similarities and differences of, 50–53

students' behavior, as indicator of deep engagement, 39

Study Driven: A Framework for Planning Units of Study in the Writing Workshop (Ray), 50

Sulzby, Elizabeth, 85

system, learning writing as interrelated, 16, 18

talk
    dramatic play and favorite read-alouds as supporting oral language development, 91
    importance of, 31–32
    as indicator of deep engagement, 39